A Brave New Series

GLOBAL ISSUES
IN A CHANGING WORLD

This new series of short, accessible think-pieces deals with leading global issues of relevance to humanity today. Intended for the enquiring reader and social activists in the North and the South, as well as students, the books explain what is at stake and question conventional ideas and policies. Drawn from many different parts of the world, the series' authors pay particular attention to the needs and interests of ordinary people, whether living in the rich industrial or the developing countries. They all share a common objective: to help stimulate new thinking and social action in the opening years of the new century.

Global Issues in a Changing World is a joint initiative by Zed Books in collaboration with a number of partner publishers and non-governmental organizations around the world. By working together, we intend to maximize the relevance and availability of the books published in the series.

Participating NGOs

Both ENDS, Amsterdam
Catholic Institute for International Relations, London
Corner House, Sturminster Newton
Council on International and Public Affairs, New York
Dag Hammarskjöld Foundation, Uppsala
Development GAP, Washington DC
Focus on the Global South, Bangkok
IBON: Manila
Inter Pares, Ottawa
Public Interest Research Centre, Delhi
Third World Network, Penang
Third World Network–Africa, Accra
World Development Movement, London

About this series

Communities in the South are facing great difficulties in coping with global trends. I hope this brave new series will throw much-needed light on the issues ahead and help us choose the right options.

Martin Khor, Director, Third World Network, Penang

There is no more important campaign than our struggle to bring the global economy under democratic control. But the issues are fearsomely complex. This Global Issues series is a valuable resource for the committed campaigner and the educated citizen.

Barry Coates, Director, Oxfam New Zealand

Zed Books has long provided an inspiring list about the issues that touch and change people's lives. The Global Issues series is another dimension of Zed's fine record, allowing access to a range of subjects and authors that, to my knowledge, very few publishers have tried. I strongly recommend these new, powerful titles and this exciting series.

John Pilger, author

We are all part of a generation that actually has the means to eliminate extreme poverty worldwide. Our task is to harness the forces of globalization for the benefit of working people, their families and their communities – that is our collective duty. The Global Issues series makes a powerful contribution to the global campaign for justice, sustainable and equitable development, and peaceful progress.

Glenys Kinnock MEP

About the author

Peggy Antrobus was born in Grenada and educated there and in St Lucia and St Vincent. She holds a bachelor's degree in economics, a professional certificate in social work and a doctorate in education. She has been employed in government and NGO programmes in St Vincent, Jamaica and Barbados.

Since 1974, when she was appointed as Advisor on Women's Affairs to the Government of Jamaica, she has worked in the field of Women in Development. In 1987 she set up the Women and Development Unit (WAND) within the School of Continuing Studies at the University of the West Indies (UWI) and was its head until her retirement in 1995.

She was a founding member of CAFRA (the Caribbean Association for Feminist Research and Action). She was also a founding member of DAWN, the network of Third World women promoting Development Alternatives with Women for a New Era; its Coordinator 1990–96; and on its Steering Committee 1990–2004.

She has written and spoken on a number of topics related to the issues of women and development, and women's organizing, and has contributed to various publications on these topics.

Her recent work focuses on the impact of government policies on women, and the ways in which these policies reflect global trends. She has a special interest in transformational leadership in the women's movement. She describes women who exhibit this kind of leadership as feminists with a passion for justice and a commitment to change things and change themselves.

PEGGY ANTROBUS

The Global Women's Movement
Origins, issues and strategies

University Press Ltd
DHAKA

White Lotus Co. Ltd
BANGKOK

Fernwood Publishing Ltd
NOVA SCOTIA

Ian Randle Publishers
KINGSTON

Books for Change
BANGALORE

SIRD
KUALA LUMPUR

David Philip
CAPE TOWN

Zed Books
LONDON · NEW YORK

The Global Women's Movement: Origins, issues and strategies was first published in 2004 by:

in Bangladesh: The University Press Ltd, Red Crescent Building, 14 Motijheel C/A, PO Box 2611, Dhaka 1000

in Burma, Cambodia, Laos, Thailand and Vietnam: White Lotus Co. Ltd, GPO Box 1141, Bangkok 10501, Thailand

in Canada: Fernwood, 8422 St Margaret's Bay Road (Hwy 3), Site 2A, Box 5, Black Point, Nova Scotia B0J 1B0

in the Caribbean: Ian Randle Publishers, 11 Cunningham Avenue, PO Box 686, Kingston 6, Jamaica

in India: Books for Change, 139 Richmond Road, Bangalore 560 025

in Malaysia: Strategic Information Research Department (SIRD), No. 11/4E Petaling Jaya, 46200 Selangor

in Southern Africa: David Philip Publishers (Pty Ltd), 99 Garfield Road, Claremont 7700, South Africa

in the rest of the world: Zed Books Ltd, 7 Cynthia Street, London N1 9JF, UK and Room 400, 175 Fifth Avenue, New York, NY 10010, USA

www.zedbooks.co.uk

Copyright © Peggy Antrobus, 2004

The right of Peggy Antrobus to be identified as the author of this work has been asserted by her in accordance with the Copyright, Designs and Patents Act, 1988

Cover designed by Andrew Corbett
Set in Monotype Dante and Gill Sans Heavy by Ewan Smith, London
Printed and bound in the United Kingdom by Cox & Wyman, Reading

Distributed in the USA exclusively by Palgrave, a division of St Martin's Press, LLC, 175 Fifth Avenue, New York, NY 10010

A catalogue record for this book is available from the British Library
US CIP data is available from the Library of Congress
Canadian CIP data is available from the National Library of Canada

ISBN 1 55266 153 9 pb (Canada)
ISBN 976 637 209 8 pb (Caribbean)
ISBN 81 8291 005 6 pb (India)
ISBN 983 2535 43 3 pb (Malaysia)
ISBN 1 84277 016 0 hb (Zed Books)
ISBN 1 84277 017 9 pb (Zed Books)

Contents

Abbreviations and acronyms

AAWORD	African Association for Women's Research and Development
AWID	Association for Women's Rights and Development
CSOs	Civil society organizations
CWGL	Center for Women's Global Leadership (based in Rutgers University, USA)
DAWN	Development Alternatives with Women for a New Era
FIRE	Feminist International Radio Endeavor (based in Costa Rica)
GNP	Gross national product
IAFE	International Association for Feminist Economics
ICPD	International Conference on Population and Development
IFIs	International financial institutions (e.g. the World Bank)
IGTN	International Gender and Trade Network
IMF	International Monetary Fund
IWD	International Women's Day (8 March)
IWTC	International Women's Tribune Centre
IWY	International Women's Year (1975)
NGO	Non-governmental organization
NIEO	New International Economic Order
SAPs	Structural Adjustment Programmes
UNCED	UN Conference on Environment and Development
UNIFEM	United Nations Development Fund for Women
UNFPA	UN Fund for Population Activities
WAND	Women and Development Unit (based at the University of the West Indies)
WEDO	Women's Environment and Development Organization
WEF	World Economic Forum
WID	Women in development
WSF	World Social Forum
WTO	World Trade Organization

Acknowledgements and biographical note

This book is shaped by a particular perspective – mine. Growing up in the small islands of the West Indies during the 1940s in a family of public servants, I had first-hand experience of the social and political processes leading up to adult suffrage and independence from Britain. My decision to read for a degree in economics in 1953 reflected my understanding that economic development was the other side of the coin of political independence.

Working in the field of socio-economic development from the 1950s onwards, I found myself engaged in the implementation of many of the prevailing development strategies of the time: national planning in the 1950s (with the Jamaica Planning Unit); community development and applied nutrition programmes in the 1960s (with the Save the Children Fund and the Government of St Vincent respectively); Women in Development in the 1970s (as Director of the Jamaica Women's Bureau); women's empowerment from the 1980s onwards with the Women and Development Unit (WAND) within the School of Continuing Studies of the University of the West Indies. Over this period I worked with governments and NGOs, in local communities, and at national, regional and international levels.

In August 1984 I was one of a small group of women who met to prepare a platform document and a series of panels for the NGO Forum that paralleled the 1985 Third UN Conference on Women to be held in Nairobi. The success of these panels led to the launching of the network of Third World feminists, Development Alternatives with Women for a New Era (DAWN). DAWN reflects Third World women's challenge to the dominant development model, the 'growth' model, and this conceptual framework was to influence my thinking and analysis profoundly. Any DAWN publications referred to in the book can be traced via the DAWN website – see p. 189.

Involvement in programmes within the UN Decade for Women (1975–85) changed my work and life. Exposure to UN conferences and processes was a learning experience more profound than reading for university degrees. But it was exposure to feminism in the second half of the Decade that was transformative. It changed my understanding of political economy, my professional practice and my politics.

This book has been influenced by many women whose friendship, support and ideas have shaped my thinking over the past forty years. First I acknowledge Lucille Mair, who opened the door to my involvement in the women's movement, seeing in me someone who could create a programme for the advancement of women within the Jamaican bureaucracy. I learned about feminism from two sources: working-class Jamaican women who showed me that privileges of class and education could also be constraints, and women in the leadership of the international women's movement in the Decade for Women – Charlotte Bunch, who helped me to see the relevance of feminism to economics and colonialism; Adrienne Germain (then at the Ford Foundation) and Kristin Anderson (at the Carnegie Corporation), who helped me see the significance of my work; Ann Walker and Vicky Semler at the International Women's Tribune Centre; Bella Abzug at the UN; Angela Miles and Linda Christensen-Ruffman of Canada; Nita Barrow, Audrey Roberts, Andaiye, Joan French, Rhoda Reddock and Eudine Barriteau of the Caribbean; Judith Bruce and Genevieve Vaughn of the USA, and the many talented, imaginative and courageous women with whom I worked at WAND (1978–95).

I am especially indebted to Nan Peacocke, who helped me understand my own power, to the women of DAWN, and countless others whose friendship and support helped me grow.

In the final stage of writing I tested the manuscript with the students of Linda Ruffman's women's studies class at the University of St Mary's in Halifax, Canada. Their endorsement of certain elements in the book – the use of boxes for personal reflection and the imagery used to describe the women's movement in Chapter 2 – indicated that I was on the right track.

More recently I encountered the young women of the DAWN Training Institute in Feminist Advocacy. Their knowledge, passion and creativity inspired me and gave me clarity about the audience for whom this book is intended.

To these young women, to all the women whose friendship and support have helped me grow, and to the grassroots women of Haiti I dedicate this book.

Peggy Antrobus
Barbados

Preface

It took me some time to recognize that I was being offered an incredible gift when Robert Molteno invited me to write this book on the worldwide women's movement as part of Zed Books' Global Issues Series, 'for a new generation of activists'. My enthusiastic acceptance of the offer was related more to satisfaction that the topic was to be included in the series than to feelings that I was capable of writing it. Then came 11 September 2001, and in the turmoil and trauma of the events I realized that I wanted to write this book. There is something a global women's movement has to offer to our understanding of what happened, and to the steps that must be taken to break the cycle of violence and injustice. Finally, I realized that I did indeed have something to share; that this rich experience of a journey in consciousness that took me from working as an economist, social worker and bureaucrat in the field of development, to participation in a movement for global justice focused on women's perspectives and agency, was the very stuff of this book.

The war in Iraq compels us to recognize that we are in a most dangerous conjuncture of relentless neo-liberalism, virulent religious and ideological fundamentalisms, aggressive militarism and resurgent racism. That an impressive mobilization of, and massive demonstrations by, civil society could not stop the war has introduced a necessary dose of humility; but the brutalizing displays of patriarchal definitions of masculinity in Washington and Baghdad have reinforced my view that another world is possible only if we confront the patriarchal (and racist) roots of our present crises.

As I approached the completion of the final manuscript, the February 2004 crisis in Haiti caused me to think again of the limitations of a movement based solely on gender identity, and of the vulnerability of civil society to manipulation by forces that oppose social justice. The confrontation of contradictions and complexity is central to an assessment of the potential of women's movements as a force for transformation towards a better world for all.

My perspective on the topic is one of many. Each person has his or her own experience of this movement that addresses, however inadequately, the key issues that affect our survival as a human species. It is my view that in its rejection of dichotomies; its linking of the personal to the political, the household to the economy, the rational to the intuitive; its on-going struggles to confront divisions of race and ethnicity, class and nationality; its validation of women's work, experience and agency, and especially in the value it places on tolerance, diversity and solidarity, a feminist-led global women's movement has the political means to contribute to our understanding of the crises that confront us, and to the solutions that must be found.

1 | Introduction

A book about a global women's movement is, inevitably, controversial. The adjective 'global' itself appears to minimize cultural and contextual differences that are valued by women's movements in different cultures and contexts, and indeed to disregard profound differences among women even within national boundaries. Realities of class, race, nationality, ethnicity, geographical location, age, sexual orientation, physical capacity, religion and political affiliation often lead to sharp divisions.

As someone involved in many of the processes that have led to the construction of this worldwide movement, and a witness to the ways in which it has changed since the 1970s, largely through the influence of Third World feminists and women of colour in North America, I am amazed to find that its image remains one of a movement associated with white, middle-class women from North America and Europe. I welcome this opportunity, therefore, to write about the process through which the movement has been transformed over forty years from a rich diversity of local movements into an international women's movement and finally into a trans-national or global movement.

Now more than ever, I affirm the need for such a movement as we search urgently for paths through 'our fragmented yet globally interdependent world'[1] to find the solutions to the many threats to human survival, well-being and security. The primary question that this book attempts to answer is this: is there a global women's movement, and what might it contribute, through the overarching social movement for global justice, to finding alternative paths that would make 'another world' possible?

To answer that question I consider the origins of a movement formed out of many movements shaped in local struggles and brought together in the context of global opportunities and challenges. I reflect on the trajectory of the emerging movement

I

as women discover commonalities and come to a better understanding of how the social relations of gender are implicated in the systemic crises that have contributed to persistent poverty, social exclusion and alienation, environmental deterioration and the spread of violence that threatens the well-being and security of the majority of the world's people and the planet itself.

One of the problems with a book of this nature is the need to simplify complex issues and to reach conclusions about those that are still the subject of debate. As I complete the task I am more acutely aware of this and have to remind myself that no amount of extra time, or rewriting, can circumvent this problem.

While other books in this series deal in greater detail with the major socio-economic and political events of the past forty years,[2] it is important to remember both the different ways in which these events have impacted on women and the specific contribution that women's perspectives have made to shaping the debates and agendas. Women's experiences are therefore located within the broader context of these global trends and challenges.

Zed Books has also recently published a number of other titles related to the subject of women's movements. Special mention must be made of two, *Common Ground or Mutual Exclusion? Women's Movements and International Relations*, a collection of papers presented at a symposium of the same name, held at the University of Frankfurt am Main, Germany, 30 June–2 July 2000, edited by Marianne Braig and Sonja Wolte, and *Feminist Futures: Re-imagining Women, Culture and Development* edited by Kum-Kum Bhavnani, John Foran and Priya Kurian (2003). These titles touch on many themes in my book, while their differences make them complementary. As a single-authored book, mine carries the flaws, or advantages, of subjectivity. It is also less academic and more personal, having been written by one who has also been a participant in the shaping of the global movement. In that sense, it lacks the depth and breadth of the other books, and I urge those who wish to get a fuller sense of the strengths and limitations of women's movements at various levels and in different spaces to read these and many other books on the subject. I found them challenging and inspiring and I have engaged some of the issues they raise.

At the start of the 21st century we are witnessing a consolidation of economic, political and social power on an unprecedented scale. The values, institutional processes and motivational imperatives around materialistic individualism accompanying the explosion and concentration of capital are a threat to the well-being of the majority of the world's peoples and cultures and to the ecological integrity of our planet. The war in Iraq has highlighted the extreme danger posed when processes of power consolidation are embodied in a single ideology-driven super-power that evokes in response an equally virulent and violent form of religious fundamentalism. The resulting conjuncture of relentless neo-liberalism, virulent religious and ideological fundamentalism, aggressive militarism and resurgent racism poses particular dangers for women and for people of colour worldwide, and calls for a clearer integration, in the work of the emerging social movement for global justice, of an analysis of the sexism and racism underlying these processes and forces.

The evolution of geo-political events over the last century can be tracked by the pattern of social movements that emerged to challenge the most extreme forms of capitalist exploitation, militarism, dictatorship, sexism and racism. Nationalist and often regional in character, these movements were cognisant of both the global histories of their local circumstances and of the global causes manifest in their related struggles. They include movements against colonialism, imperialism, dictatorship and racism; on behalf of labour; and movements for women's liberation.

In the first half of the 20th century, independence, democracy and socialism offered visions of alternatives to colonialism, authoritarianism and capitalism around the world. The decades of the 1960s and 1970s saw the first glimmers of hope for postcolonial peoples, formalized in the promises of the UN Development Decades, North–South Dialogues and calls for a New International Economic Order (NIEO). In the past thirty years, since the collapse of the socialist alternative, new social movements are again emerging to challenge the excesses of unregulated capitalism.

Emerging out of the demonstrations that took place in Seattle around the Second Ministerial Meeting of the World Trade

Organization (WTO) in November 1999, and facilitated by advances in information and communications technologies, a social movement, initially named the 'anti-globalization' movement,[3] has been gathering strength. The spread of neo-liberalism as expressed through the operations of the WTO and the international financial institutions (IFIs) was challenged wherever representatives of these organizations and those of the eight most powerful governments (the G-8)[4] met in the years following Seattle.[5] Since that time these groups have begun to consolidate around the World Social Forum (WSF), initiated in January 2001 by Brazilian and European NGOs to counter the World Economic Forum (WEF) that had been meeting annually in Davos, Switzerland, for over thirty years. The WSF, meeting for the first time outside Brazil,[6] seems destined to be the coming together of social movements of the first decade of this new century. It is not a single movement but a 'movement of movements', an unprecedented alliance that has been growing around a diversity of issues over the past twenty years.

Catalysed by the UN conferences of the 1980s and 1990s, environmentalists, feminists and human rights activists have been joined by reinvigorated movements from the 1950s and 1960s – trade unionists, activists from the civil rights and peace movements, anarchists and liberation theologians. Following the collapse of the Marxist parties of the former Soviet Union and its socialist allies, these movements, many of them originating in leftist politics, have found new meaning in struggles for social justice around issues related to the political economy of neo-liberalism and corporate-led globalization. Uniting this diversity of agendas, politics and strategies is a common resistance to the spread of neo-liberalism, which privileges the interests of capital over the needs and aspirations of people, and is managed through the operations of the IFIs, the WTO and the UN.

At the World Social Forum, 2003, tens of thousands of participants, from over 150 countries and 5,000 organizations,[7] offered an analysis that linked the difficulties surrounding WTO negotiations, the recession following the widespread failure of technology stocks in 2001, the bankruptcy and corruption of the Enron corporation,[8] and the collapse of Argentina's economy early in

2002, to the failure of neo-liberalism's promise of growth and prosperity for all. They also saw how this related to the US war in Afghanistan and the 'war against terrorism', the profits that the arms and energy corporations were poised to make from these wars, and the suffering they would inflict on poor people. At the 2002 Forum, a campaign against fundamentalisms – 'all of them', economic and political no less than religious – organized by Latin American women's movements, highlighted the ways in which women's lives and livelihoods are jeopardized by the convergences between the different social, economic, political and cultural processes unleashed or exacerbated by neo-liberalism.

Latin American women's movements are part of a worldwide women's movement that has been building over the past twenty-five years. Nurtured and energized by the processes of the UN Decade for Women (1975–85) and emerging in the context of the UN global conferences of the 1990s, representatives of women's activist networks from around the world have begun shaping a recognizable global women's movement. Their analyses, perspectives, methods of organizing and strategizing, bring new dimensions to the processes of international negotiation on issues of socio-economic development, environment, human rights, population, poverty, trade and governance. As members of non-governmental organizations (NGOs) as well as through their own organizations, women are a dynamic part of the global civil society that confronts the challenges of corporate-led globalization today. Moreover, given the gender division of labour, these challenges speak to issues of special concern to women.

This book affirms the global women's movement, its agendas and strategies and its potential for bringing new perspectives to the current global struggles for peace and social justice. In Chapter 2, I attempt a definition, and identify and analyse its origins in local movements that have arisen from specific national struggles around issues of citizenship, rights and participation. While women's international activism undoubtedly preceded the First World War, I have chosen to place this book in the context of the UN Decade for Women and the period following, up to the current time (2004). I have used this framework not only because

5

I lived this history, but because the framework allows us to see clearly how such a movement took shape both in terms of its geographical spread and its evolving theory and practice around issues that have become increasingly global.

Chapters 3 and 4 review the debates about socio-economic development in the context of the UN's First and Second Development Decades of the 1960s and 1970s (Chapter 3) and the UN Decade for Women (Chapter 4).

In Chapter 4, I discuss the ways in which the UN Decade for Women created spaces that brought together women of diverse backgrounds. Women from traditional women's organizations and grassroots organizations of all kinds, feminist-oriented groups, researchers and women involved in policy formulation and programme implementation, created a movement that can be described as 'international'. The chapter shows how the designation by the UN of 1975 as International Women's Year (IWY) galvanized a decade characterized by debates on equity and participation; how it prepared women to respond to the crises of the decade of the 1980s, and to participate in the larger arenas of the global conferences of the 1990s.

Chapter 5 focuses on the decade of the 1980s, the Decade of Adjustment, described by many Latin Americans as the 'lost decade'. The dedication of a whole chapter to this decade indicates its significance for women's movements in many countries of the South, and ultimately for women's movements and social movements everywhere. Feminist analyses of the impact of the IMF-inspired structural adjustment policies that provided the policy framework during this decade, as well as women's responses to the socio-economic and political crises provoked by their introduction, led to new insights as to the ways in which assumptions about gender roles were embedded in public policies. This in turn opened the way to new forms of organizing and analysis that were to place women in a position to bring new perspectives to the global debates of the 1990s.

Chapter 6 examines the emergence of a trans-national or global women's movement in the context of the global conferences of the 1990s around issues of environment, human rights, population and poverty. It shows how the articulation of an analysis drawn from the experiences of the most marginalized women facilitated a shift from 'women's issues' to women's perspectives on a range of issues of concern to everyone. In addition to the differences among women, the discussion will show how the positions advanced by women differed from those of their governments and of male-dominated NGOs and social movements. The chapter will identify the ways in which the participation of this global women's movement changed the terms and outcomes of global debates.

Chapter 7 looks critically at the political strategies and dynamics of women's organizations and feminist activism over the period covered by this book, and reflects on the lessons learned.

Chapter 8 considers the challenges and dilemmas facing the global women's movement in the 21st century.

Chapter 9 considers the kind of leadership needed for moving forward. The issue is, how might a global women's movement strengthen and renew itself in order to contribute to finding ways out of this troubling conjuncture of forces that poses particular threats to the security of women and people of colour.

An Epilogue reflects on the implications for women's movements of the experiences of Iraq and Haiti. It places the US-led war against Iraq in the context of the enduring sexism and racism that underlie the current crisis in human security, while arguing that Haiti teaches us the limitations of a movement that focuses on gender identity without considering the ways in which differences of class, power and race create deep divisions among women.

This book is part of Zed Books' Global Issues Series. The reader may refer to other titles on the prevailing global system that, in the words of their descriptive material, is 'unsustainable in environmental terms; unstable and inequitable in economic terms; and biased against development prospects for countries in the South'. The inclusion of a book on the global women's movement in this series points to Zed's understanding of the significance of this movement within a large process that seeks to assist a new generation of activists in their search for alternatives that will lead to a better world for all.

Notes

1 Charlotte Bunch's endorsement of Amrita Basu's *Challenge of Local Feminisms*, 1995 (see Bibliography).

2 These include: Nicholas Guyatt (*Another American Century*) on how US policy shaped the discourse on development, John Madeley (*Hungry for Trade*) on trade, and Martin Khor (*Globalization*) on the impact of globalization on the economies of the South. (See list after the Index, this volume.)

3 The current title, the 'movement for global justice', comes closer to capturing the wider agenda of the movement.

4 These include the USA, Canada, the UK, France, Germany, Italy, Russia and Japan.

5 The site of the 2nd Ministerial Meeting of the WTO.

6 In Mumbai, India, from 16–24 January 2004.

7 Of these it was estimated that 15,084 were delegates and 15,000 were living in the youth camp. Fifty-seven per cent of the delegates were male and 43 per cent female.

8 The Enron corporation was one of the five largest energy corporations in the USA with links to both the White House and Congress.

2 | The global women's movement: definitions and local origins

The authors of this Kenya case study describe a process which is common to many of us as we are called on to consider the question of whether there is a women's movement. This chapter attempts to answer the questions: Is there a global women's movement? How can we understand such a movement? How can it be defined, and what are its characteristics? My conclusion is that there is a global women's movement. It is different from other social movements and can be defined by diversity, its feminist politics and perspectives, its global reach and its methods of organizing.

Definitions

In her book, commissioned by the Ford Foundation as a contribution to the events surrounding the Fourth World Conference on Women held in Beijing in September 1995, Amrita Basu put together a collection of writings documenting the manifestations

---

Personal reflection

When we were first approached about writing on the women's movement in Kenya, one question emerged in both of our minds: Is there a women's movement in Kenya? When we considered this, we simultaneously answered, 'No'. After more reflection, we began to ask, 'If there is no women's movement, what is this intense activity going on around us of women's group meetings, workshops, seminars, and even individual women agitating for women's rights in the courts, in the media and even on the streets? (*Wilhelmina Oduol and Wanjiku Mukabi Kabira*).[1]

---

of feminist politics through local struggles which shape and are shaped by feminism. She defines women's movements as comprising 'a range of struggles by women against gender inequality'. The seventeen case studies, from as many countries or regions, describe and analyse a rich diversity of experience, grounded in specific local struggles.[2]

Many authors admit that this movement does not conform to conventional definitions of a 'movement', lacking as it does common objectives, continuity, unity and coordination. Yet this should not surprise us, nor should it be taken as a sign of deficiency. Women's movements are, after all, different from all other social movements in that they are crosscutting, ask different questions, and often seek goals that challenge conventional definitions of where we want to go.[3] Only a few activists take the view that the objectives of the women's movement are similar to those of labour, human rights and student groups, which seek justice for their members. Many see the objectives of women's groups as broader, seeking changes in relationships that are more varied and complex. At the same time it is sometimes difficult to identify clear objectives; worse, the objectives articulated by some groups seem to contradict those of others. The following quotes from the Nigerian case study illustrate the problem:

> The Nigerian women's movement is an unarmed movement. It is non-confrontational. It is a movement for the progressive upliftment of women for motherhood, nationhood and development.[4]

And again:

> When African women demand equality, we are only asking for our rights not to be tampered with, and the removal of laws that oppress and dehumanize women. We are not asking for equality with our husbands. We accept them as the bosses and heads of the family.[5]

The confusion and contradictions captured in these statements reflect the complexity of a movement that is caught in the tension between what is possible and what is dreamed of, between short-term goals and long-term visions, between expediency and risk-taking, pragmatism and surrender, between the practical and the strategic. Most of all, there is understandable ambivalence surrounding challenging and confronting relationships that are intimate and deeply felt. But the confusion also reflects a lack of clarity about definitions of what groups might be considered part of a 'women's movement'.

Many activists, including Nigerian activists who identify themselves with a women's movement, would question definitions of the objectives of their movement in terms of the 'upliftment of women for motherhood, nationhood and development'. They would argue that this instrumentalizes women, while being in complete accord with patriarchal definitions of women's traditional role.

It seems to me that the continuing confusion about what defines women's movements relates not so much to the fact that this movement does not conform to a conventional definition of a movement, but rather to lack of clarity about objectives in contexts that differ widely.

One way of clarifying these apparent contradictions is to recognize two mutually reinforcing tendencies within women's movements – one focused on gender identity (identity politics) and the other concerned with a larger project for social transformation.[6] There are two entry points to concerns about a larger social project. One is recognition of the centrality of the care and nurture of human beings to the larger social project, and that to address this, given the primacy of women's gendered role in this area, requires addressing gender relations in all the complex interplay of their economic, social, political, cultural and personal dimensions. It also involves locating gender inequality within other forms of inequality that shape and often exacerbate it.

Another entry point is recognition that women cannot be separated from the larger context of their lived experience and that this includes considerations of class, race/ethnicity and geographic location, among other factors. This means that the struggle for women's agency must include engagement in struggles against sources of women's oppression that extend beyond gender.

The larger social project would therefore include transforming social institutions, practices and beliefs so that they address gender relations along with other oppressive relationships, not simply seeking a better place within existing institutions and structures. For this reason, women's movements in countries where the majority of women are marginalized by class, race or ethnicity must be concerned with the larger social project. This is often a point of tension between women's movements in the context of North–South relations, as well as in the context of struggles against oppression on the basis of class, race and ethnicity.

I believe that confusion about definitions of women's movements is also caused by failure to make distinctions between women's organizations as part of a wide spectrum of non-governmental organizations (NGOs) or civil society organizations (CSOs), and those that might be better understood as part of a politically oriented social movement.

Similarly, the term 'women's movements' is sometimes used interchangeably with 'feminist movements', an error that confuses and misrepresents both feminism and the broad spectrum of women's organizations.

In the final analysis, it seems to me that the identification of feminist politics as the engine of women's movements may help to clarify some of the confusion around women's organizing in the period covered by this book, as well as to focus the answer to the central question: Can women's movements make a difference in the struggle for equity, democracy and sustainability in today's globalized economy? It is the combination of struggles for gender justice with those for economic justice and democracy that enables women's movements to make a difference to the larger social project for transformation of systems and relationships.

An important segment of women's movements is composed of the associations that work to incorporate a feminist perspective into their theoretical, analytical, professional and political work. In academia, most disciplines now have feminist associations – Anthropology, Economics, Political, Social and Natural Sciences and Theology, among others. Moreover, within these disciplines – whether women are organized into feminist associations or not – women in the academies are doing important theoretical and empirical work that deepens our understanding of women's realities and produces the analyses and insights that strengthen the work of activists.

In the professions there are also women's associations – doctors, nurses, midwives, social workers, teachers, lawyers, bankers etc. – that are challenging patriarchal patterns and relationships, raising new questions and changing the practices and methods by which their professions operate.

Many women's organizations, even those that focus on traditional concerns of home and family, are nevertheless important participants in women's movements. Among these are grassroots women's organizations of various kinds – Women's Institutes, Federations of Women, the YWCA, and many worldwide organizations identified with strong advocacy on behalf of women's rights, although they may not describe themselves as feminist.[7]

Finally, a definition of a women's movement must include those individual women who would never join an organization, nor define themselves as feminists, but whose lives and actions nevertheless serve to advance the liberation of women in their community and beyond.

All of these women must be seen as part of, or at least contributing to, women's movements. They are all part of the diversity and richness of a movement that seeks change in the relationships of superiority and inferiority, domination and subordination between women and men in a patriarchal world.

The following statements summarize my own views on women's movements:

- A women's movement is a *political* movement – part of the broad array of social movements concerned with changing social conditions, rather than part of a network of women's organizations (although many women's organizations may be part of a women's movement).
- A women's movement is grounded in an understanding of women's relations to *social conditions* – an understanding of gender as an important relationship within the broad structure

of social relationships of class, race and ethnicity, age and location.

- A women's movement is a *process*, discontinuous, flexible, responding to specific conditions of perceived gender inequality or gender-related injustice. Its focal points may be in women's organizations, but it embraces individual women in various locations who identify with the goals of feminism at a particular point in time.

- Awareness and *rejection of patriarchal privilege* and control are central to the politics of women's movements.

- In most instances, the 'movement' is born at the moments in which individual women become aware of *their separateness as women*, their alienation, marginalization, isolation or even abandonment within a broader movement for social justice or social change. In other words, women's struggle for agency within the broader struggle is the catalyst for women's movements.

bell hooks describes this process of *conscientization* thus:

> Our search leads us back to where it all began, to that moment when an individual woman ... who may have thought she was all alone, began a feminist uprising, began to name her practice, indeed began to formulate theory from lived experience.[8]

Women from across the world who identify themselves as part of an international and global women's movement are to be found participating in international meetings organized by feminist associations, networks and organizations such as the International Inter-disciplinary Congress, the Association for Women's Rights and Development (AWID) and UN conferences.[9] They celebrate annual special 'days' such as International Women's Day (IWD) on 8 March and International Day Against Violence Against Women on 25 November. They are in constant communication with each other through the Internet, where they sign petitions and statements in solidarity with women around the world, formulate strategies and organize campaigns and meetings.

The movement has important resources:

- resource centres such as the International Women's Tribune Centre (IWTC), set up following the 1975 International Women's Year (IWY) Conference in Mexico City;
- media, such as feminist radio stations like the Costa Rica-based FIRE (Feminist International Radio Endeavor); news services like WINGS (Women's International News Gathering Service) and Women's Feature Services (WFS), supported initially by UNESCO;
- websites (see p. 189–90);
- publishers and women's presses;
- artists and artistes – filmmakers, musicians, dancers, painters, writers, poets and playwrights;
- women's funds started by individual philanthropists and organizations that support women's projects, organizations and networks.

Characteristics

Diversity Experience of the past thirty years points to the pitfall of starting with an assumption of a 'global sisterhood', especially when that 'sisterhood' is defined by a privileged minority. The emergence of a global movement has indeed depended on the emergence of new and different voices challenging hegemonic tendencies and claiming their own voice and space, and the acceptance of differences within the movements.

Diversity is now recognized as perhaps the most important characteristic of women's movements. Nevertheless, many of the tensions among women in their movements can be related to differences of race/ethnicity, nationality/culture and class, although, as Audre Lorde points out:

> [I]t is not those differences between us that are separating us. It is rather our refusal to recognize [them] and to examine the distortions which result from our misnaming them and their effects upon human behaviour and expectation.[10]

She also reminds us, 'There is no such thing as a single-issue struggle because we do not live single-issue lives.'[11] Women understand that each of us has multiple identities and that at any point in time one or other may be more important than others. Insistence on focusing on gender in isolation from issues like race, ethnicity and class has often been more divisive than the inclusion of these issues in the agendas of the various movements. It is indeed impossible and even counterproductive to separate the varied forms of oppression because of the systemic links between them. Thus in many countries of the South women have had to confront colonialism, imperialism or racism before they could confront patriarchy.

Feminist politics It may be useful to identify feminism as a specific politics, grounded in a consciousness of all the sources of women's subordination, and with a commitment to challenge and change the relationships and structures which perpetuate women's subordinate position, in solidarity with other women. The consciousness of sexism and sexist oppression is the essence of feminist politics, and it is this politics that energizes women's movements, whether or not the word 'feminist' is used. It is possible then to identify feminist politics as a specific element within a broader universe of women's organizations, women's movements and other social movements.

Feminists have worked with and within other social movements – especially those on peace, racism, the environment, indigenous peoples and the poor. These initiatives have served both to broaden and redefine the issues of concern to women, as well as to refocus the agendas of these movements.

In addition, there are feminists within institutions and agencies who recognize the ways in which the ideology of patriarchy constrains and diminishes the achievement of laudable goals and objectives, and who engage in the struggle to challenge it.

Feminist politics can also be identified within bureaucratic initiatives and institutional arrangements established for the improvement of the condition and position of women, enabling them to contribute to the movement for gender justice. These include women's bureaus, desks, commissions, special units and gender focal points within mainstream institutions.

Global reach Our understanding of the diversity within women's movements that has led us to speak more often of a multiplicity of 'movements' would lead many to question the concept of a single global women's movement. However, I would argue, as others have done, that despite the rich diversity of experience, grounded in specific local struggles, women have been able to transcend these to become a movement of global proportions, with a global agenda and perspective.

Here I want to distinguish between an international women's movement and a global women's movement.[12] Although, as Uta Ruppert has pointed out, local or national women's movements have never viewed their activities as 'simply crossing the borders of nation states',[13] I would conceptualize an 'international' movement as one in which the national and cultural differences between women were recognizable and paramount. Indeed, this was characteristic of women's movements at the international level in the mid-1970s, at the launching of the UN Decade for Women (1975–85), and to some extent throughout most of the Decade. However, as women established their separate identities along the prevailing axes of North–South, East–West, they discovered commonalities that moved them increasingly towards greater coherence and even common positions in the policy debates around issues of environment, poverty, violence and human rights. At the same time, as these issues became increasingly 'global' (as reflected in the themes and agendas of the global conferences of the 1990s), women's movements converged in these global arenas to negotiate and articulate common agendas and positions. As Ruppert puts it:

> The political process of international women's movements has been shaped by the insight that international politics does not simply take place at the inter-nation-state level, but also encompasses multicentric and multilevel processes. Thus the movement's multidimensional political understanding, which is sensitive to differences, almost predestined it to become the most global of social movements of the 1990s.[14]

She goes on to identify:

[A] second component ... essential for the women's movement to become an effective global actor, [which] was the movement's shift toward aiming for 'globality' as a main objective. Even though there has never been an explicit discourse along these lines, the movement's political practice suggests a conceptual differentiation between three different political approaches on the global level: criticizing and combating globalization as a neo-liberal paradigm; utilizing global politics, or rather global governance, as tools for governance under the conditions of globalization; and specifically creating 'globality',[15] which the women's movement has aimed for and worked towards as an important factor in women's global politics.[16]

Methods of organizing It is widely understood that a characteristic of a global women's movement is the linking of local to global, the particularities of local experience and struggles to, as Ruppert says, 'the political creation and establishment of global norms for world development and global ethics for industrial production, such as (social and gender) justice, sustainability and peace, based on the creation of globally valid fundamental human rights'.[17] However, few have related this to the particular methods of feminist organizing.

Although, as Ruppert rightly states, this practice has not been the subject of an explicit discourse, it has nevertheless been based on conscious decisions to involve women from different backgrounds and regions in the search for 'globality'. These decisions have been the result of an understanding of the ways in which global events, trends and policies impact on local experience, and in particular on the experiences of poor women in the global South.

While Ruppert and others cite women's organizing around the 1992 UN Conference on Environment and Development (UNCED) and the 1993 International Conference on Human Rights as the first signs of this kind of organizing, I would refer to the experience of the network of Third World women, DAWN, in their preparations for the Forum of the 1985 Third World Conference on Women. It was here that a conscious attempt was made to bring together local and regional experiences as the beginning of a process for the preparation of a platform document for a global event.

I speak more about this experience in Chapters 3, 4 and 5; here I merely want to use it to illustrate the feminist methodology used for the 'globalizing' of frameworks around economics, environment and rights. The starting point was a meeting at which women were invited to reflect on their experience of development over the course of the Decade for Women – from the perspective of poor women living in the economic South. In this way the final document reflected regional differences, even as it reached for a framework that revealed the linkages between these experiences. This process – which starts with testifying to local, regional, or even individual experiences ('telling our stories', 'speaking our truths'), leading to the negotiation of differences and finally to the articulation of a position that attempts to generalize, synthesize or 'globalize' the diversity of experience – was repeated in the processes leading to the global conferences on environment, human rights and population. Chapter 6 focuses on the processes around these events.

This methodology, clearly related to that of feminist consciousness-raising and Freirian *conscientization*[18] (combining reflection on personal experience with socio-political analysis to construct and generate global advocacy) has been a powerful tool for the global women's movement. Like *conscientization,* which takes specific realities 'on the ground' as the basis for social analysis that can lead to action, it is a *praxis* (process of reflection and action) that has helped to mobilize women to challenge neo-liberal and fundamentalist state policies at national and global levels. This praxis has also been a powerful tool in feminist theorizing.

To drive home one of the differences between international women's movements and a global women's movement, I want to compare this feminist method of globalizing to the process of regional meetings and consultations used by the UN in the preparation of their international conferences. The documents that feed into and emerge from these processes have to be screened and sanctioned by governments and, by their very nature, are limited

Two

in the degree to which they are able to reflect the realities of women. While the plans and platforms of action that emerge from the conferences contain many recommendations and resolutions that accord with the advocacy of women's movements, they often lack the coherence and clarity of the platforms produced by a movement unrestrained by the conventions of international diplomacy. Moreover, without the vigilance and political activism of women's movements, especially at local or national, but also at global, levels, these recommendations are meaningless to women.

This brings me to another aspect of the links between global and local – the ways in which local actors organize to defend themselves against global threats. Recognizing the relationship between global trends and local realities, women are organizing around the defence of their bodies, their livelihoods and their communities.[19] The word 'glocality' has been coined to highlight the ways in which global trends affect local experience. This recognition of a 'politics of place' poses new challenges to a global women's movement. While organizing in the defence of 'place' has the potential to be the most powerful and effective form of organizing,[20] local groups clearly need information and analysis on the broader policy frameworks that are affecting their lives. A global women's movement also needs links to this level of organizing to retain its relevance and to legitimize its advocacy.

The global women's movement is very aware that action at global level must have resonance at local, national and regional levels if it is to be meaningful to women. In this sense we need to see the global women's movement as made up of many interlocking networks. Many of the global networks have worked to strengthen their links to activities at regional, national and local levels.

A second method of organizing, which is also a strategy (to be discussed more fully in Chapter 6), is networking. Some may say that women's movements invented networking! Networking is the method used to make the vertical (local–global) as well as the horizontal (inter-regional as well as issue-specific) links that generate the analysis and the organizing underlying global action.

A third is the linking of the personal to the political, the ways in which gender identification and recognition of common experience can short-circuit difference to create a sense of solidarity. This often makes it easier for women who are strangers to each other to work together.

Symbols and images

In the final analysis, words may not be enough to enable us to understand the complexity of a global women's movement made up of such a diversity of movements. In thinking about this book, I have often been struck by the ways in which images and symbols capture the shape and structure of a global women's movement. The images and symbols that come to mind are those of the spiral, the wheel, the pyramid, the web and the patchwork quilt.

A spiral is an open-ended circle. As an adjective it is a 'winding about a centre in an enlarging or decreasing continuous cone'. As a noun, 'a plane or three-dimensional spiral curve' (*Concise Oxford Dictionary*, 1990). In both cases it captures images of continuity and change, depth and expansion – something that is identifiable yet varied.

Inuit story-telling takes the form of a spiral, a three-dimensional curve that winds about a centre in an enlarging continuous curve that allows the story-teller to start at any point and move backwards and forwards as appropriate. The story has no end. A spiral is open-ended, continuous, ever enlarging our understanding of events, our perspectives. The global women's movement can be thought of as a spiral, a process that starts at the centre (rather than at the beginning of a line) and works its way outwards, turning, arriving at what might appear to be the same point, but in reality at an expanded understanding of the same event.

A spiral is also dialectic, allowing for the organic growth of a movement of women organizing – a movement in a state of on-going evolution as consciousness expands in the process of exchanges between women, taking us backwards (to rethink and re-evaluate old positions) and forwards (to new areas of awareness).

As a number of interlocking networks, a global women's movement might also be likened to pyramids, webs and wheels. In a study of two campaigns, the campaign against breast-milk substitutes in Ghana, and against child labour in the carpet industry in India, the New Economics Foundation (NEF) identified

> three structures for organizing constructive collaboration: the pyramid, the wheel, and the web. Pyramids have a coordinating secretariat who disseminates information through the campaign; wheels have one or more focal points for information exchange, but information also flows directly among the members; in the web, no focal point exist, so information flows to and from all the members in roughly equal quantities.[21]

The pyramid, the wheel and the web underline the fluidity of the global women's movement, comprised as it is of interlocking networks that come together as appropriate, even as each continues to focus on its specific area of interest.

Gita Sen's description of the three waves of the women's movement

The first wave had three distinct sources. One source was in the colonized countries with the emergence of social reform movements that had as their primary focus the transformation of cultural practices affecting civil laws, marriage, and family life. While these reform attempts mobilized possibly as many or more men as women, they were an important early strand in the transformation of social discourse and practice affecting gender relations. A second source was the major debate within the social democratic and communist organizations of the late nineteenth and early twentieth centuries, which then carried forward into the debates in the Soviet Union on the 'woman question'. This strand of debate was the most explicit about the connections between the institutions of private property, the control over material assets, and women–men relations within families and society. A third source was the liberal strand that combined the struggle for the vote with the struggle to legalize contraception; this strand existed mainly, though by no means exclusively, in Europe and North America.

The movement can also be understood as a patchwork quilt, full of colour and different patterns, discontinuous and defying description, but none the less an identifiable entity made up of units that have their own integrity. A quilt, an art form peculiarly developed by women, uses whatever material is available to make something both beautiful and functional. It represents ingenuity, creativity, caring and comfort. A global women's movement can have no better symbol as it seeks to create a world in which people might find beauty, comfort and security.

Origins

Since the concept of a global women's movement conceals the actors who make it possible, I turn now to consider some of the contexts that energized the local struggles out of which a global

The second wave, in the mid-twentieth century, was dominated by struggles against colonial domination, in which women were present in large numbers. Their experiences in these struggles shaped their attitudes to global economic and political inequality, even though specific issues of gender justice took a back seat at this time. Many women also went through the experience of being in the thick of anti-colonial struggles and then being marginalized in the postcolonial era.

The third wave, that we understand as the modern women's movement, had its roots in the social and political ferment of the 1960s, like so many other social movements of the later twentieth century. The anti-imperialist and anti-Vietnam War movements, civil rights struggles, challenges to social and sexual mores and behaviour, and above all the rising up of young people, brewed a potent mixture from which emerged many of the social movements of the succeeding decades worldwide. What was specific to the women's movement among these was its call for recognition of the personal as political.[22]

movement was formed. Reference is often made to 'three waves' of the women's movement: the first wave of the late 19th–early 20th century, the second covering the mid-20th century, and the third, the late 20th century. Although these waves are often depicted as distinct, it is instructive to look at the connections between them because, as Gita Sen points out:

> They delineate in an early form potential strengths as well as tensions that characterize the international women's movement right until today. The presence of multiple strands from early on has made for a movement that is broad and capable of addressing a wide range of issues. But the potential tensions between prioritizing economic issues (such as control over resources and property) or women's personal autonomy or bodily integrity existed then and continue to exist now.[23]

Conclusion

It is clear that, despite the lack of clear and common objectives, continuity, unity and coordination – characteristics that would make a women's movement identifiable with other social movements – there is nevertheless an identifiable movement enriched by its diversity and complexity, sustained by the depth of its passions and enduring commitment to its causes, and strengthened by the apparent lack of coordination and spontaneity of its strategizing.

Varied experiences highlight the complexity of women's struggles, the interplay between race, class and gender and the need to distinguish between the material and the ideological relations of gender.[24]

There are many roads to the awareness that manifests as involvement in a women's organization or identification as part of a women's movement. There are still more steps towards a feminist consciousness, which would transform involvement in a women's organization into a political struggle for gender equity and equality, often within a broader project for social transformation. Many of the women involved in women's organizations, or movements, were influenced by leftist politics, and discovered their own marginalization within the processes of these struggles. Others began the journey to feminist consciousness through personal experiences; still others through their work experience. A characteristic of many of those involved in women's movements is the process of personal transformation which they undergo as they become aware of gender subordination. At the same time, this essentially individualistic experience seems to engender a connection to the wider universe of injustice in a way that leads to a better understanding of the link between different forms of oppression and builds life-long commitments to the struggle against injustice.

Given these histories, there is no doubt that there is a global women's movement, recognizable in its understanding of how 'common difference'[25] links us all in a political struggle for recognition and redistributive justice. Its difference from other social movements lies not only in the absence of homogeneity and its lack of common objectives, continuity, unity and coordination, but in the value it places on diversity, its commitment to solidarity with women everywhere, its feminist politics and its methods of organizing.

The following chapters will explore in greater depth the contexts in which this social movement emerged and took shape, as well as examine its potential as an important global actor in the struggles for a more equitable, humane, sustainable and secure world.

Notes

1 In Basu (1995), p. 187.

2 See also Bonnie G. Smith's book, *Global Feminisms Since 1945*, published in 2000.

3 An ancient saying attributed to the Chinese states: 'If you don't change direction, you will end up where you're headed.' Where most conventional social movements are headed is still towards a place where the male is considered the definition of the human being.

4 Interview with representatives of the National Commission for Women, Abuja, 2 February 1993, Basu (1995), p. 211.

5 Interview with Obiageli Nwankwo, project coordinator, International Federation of Women Lawyers, Enugu, 1993, Basu (1995), p. 212.

6 I am grateful to Gita Sen for this analysis, which is developed in a chapter on 'The Politics of the International Women's Movement' in the book *Claiming Global Power: Transnational Civil Society and Global Governance*, edited by Srilatha Batliwala and David Brown, to be published by Kumarian Press.

7 However, there may be self-defined feminists among their members.

8. hooks (1994), p. 75.

9 Although UN conferences are also attended by women and organizations that are opposed to advances in women's human rights, as was seen at the Five-Year Review of the Fourth World Conference on Women, when the call went out from right-wing religion-based organizations for women to come to New York to 'defend' women against that 'dangerous' document, the Beijing Plan of Action.

10 Lorde (1984), p. 115.

11 Ibid., p. 138.

12 In thinking about this distinction I have found Uta Ruppert's analysis (Braig and Wolte 2002: 147–54) extremely helpful.

13 Ibid., p. 148.

14 Ibid., p. 149.

15 Ruppert defines 'globality' as 'everything global politics or global governance should be based on or directly accompanied by' (ibid., p. 151).

16 Ibid., p. 151.

17 Ibid.

18 The combination of consciousness and action, 'praxis', introduced by the Brazilian educator, Paolo Freire, to enable oppressed groups to gain an understanding of the forces impinging on their world, the sources of their oppression.

19 *Journal of the Society for International Development* (SID) on 'The Politics of Place', 2001.

20 Examples abound. The work of the Chipko movement and of the Self-Employed Women's Association (India) (SEWA) immediately come to mind because they have been so well documented; however there are examples of this kind of organizing in every region. The most recent was the action of local women in Nigeria to challenge the Shell oil company.

21 Jennifer Chapman (2001), 'What Makes International Campaigns Effective? Lessons from India and Ghana', in Edwards and Gaventa, pp. 263–4.

22 See chapter on 'The Politics of the International Women's Movement' in Srilatha Batliwala and David Brown's book cited in note 6, above.

23 Ibid.

24 Eudine Barriteau makes this distinction to show that while advances in women's material needs (practical gender interests) might be met within a policy framework of social equity based on race and class, the ideological relations of gender could cause men to resent and resist advances in terms of women's strategic gender interests.

25 Moharty and Alexander (1997). The term 'common difference' is the title of Gloria Joseph's book, and is associated with Chandra Moharty's writings.

3 | Global contexts for an emerging movement: the UN Development Decades, 1960s–1970s

Just as many of the women participating in the conferences of the Decade for Women were influenced by local struggles around issues of citizenship rights and participation, so too the Decade itself must be seen in the context of international debates around issues of citizenship, socio-economic development and redistributive justice raised by the human rights and the anti-colonial movements. However, while it is common to think of women's movements in the context of the human rights movement,[1] insufficient attention is paid to their origins in the anti-colonial and independence movements in the countries of the economic South. This is necessary if one is to understand the perspectives of those whose leadership transformed a movement that was identified with North American and European feminism into a global movement.

This chapter will deal with the international debates on socio-economic development that took place during the UN Development Decades of the 1960s and the 1970s that shaped the Decade for Women, as well as the shift in policy frameworks between the 1980s and 1990s that shaped the emerging global women's movement. These decades will be discussed in Chapters 5 and 6.

My primary questions in this chapter will be: What were the international forces and trends that led the international community to take an interest in the role and status of women, resulting in the declaration of IWY (1975) and the UN Decade for Women (1975–1985)?; and: What was the context in which international women's movements evolved into a global women's movement?

International debates on socio-economic development (1960s–1970s)

The themes of the Decade for Women – Equality, Development and Peace – were often thought to reflect the interests of the three power blocs within the UN – 'equality', the focus of the Western democracies; 'development', that of Third World countries (the economic South); and 'peace', that of the Soviet bloc. But they were also consistent with an international climate of concern and cooperation between states on issues of equity in development that characterized the 1970s. It is interesting to reflect on the fact that International Women's Year (IWY) occurred in the middle of this decade.

International interest in socio-economic and political development was heightened by the expansion of UN membership by representatives of the governments of the newly independent countries of Africa, Asia and the Caribbean. Discussions on socio-economic development within the UN and its specialized agencies reflected the concerns of these governments with improving the standards of living of their populations – the other side of the coin of independence – and led to the launching of the First Development Decade in the 1960s.

The theories underlying the strategies proposed in the UN Programme of Action of the First Development Decade were those of neo-classical economics. These theories held that the wealth generated from economic growth would trickle down to the poor and thus reduce poverty.[2] In this formulation the market was assumed to be the engine of economic growth, and although the UN provided a forum for international debate on these issues, the World Bank played the major role in promoting the strategies and generating the increases in foreign assistance (aid) which financed many of them.

The Bank itself had been set up in the second half of the 1940s as one of the international financial institutions (IFIs) mandated by a conference held at Bretton Woods in 1944 to formulate the rules and institutions by which the post-war economy would be managed. Its primary role was to make loans to developing countries to promote socio-economic development.

With its emphasis on industrialization as the path to economic growth, the role of the market was seen as critical to this process, while the role of the state was to create the physical infrastructure[3] and fiscal incentives[4] in support of market-led economic growth. In Latin America and the Caribbean, governments embarked on import-substitution industrialization (ISI) and passed legislation to encourage foreign investment in this sector. The World Bank also encouraged increases in international aid, and countries were invited to commit 0.7 per cent of their GNP to aid developing countries. The 1960s therefore saw an unprecedented increase in the flow of international aid.

However, by the end of the decade it was clear that the market by itself could not reduce poverty, and that these strategies had not achieved their objectives. Acknowledgement of the limitations of this model of market-led growth for reducing poverty led to a shift in the strategies for the Second Development Decade (1970s). These focused on the role of the state in promoting equitable and balanced development and on development planning. This approach to policy formulation,[5] which balanced the imperatives of economic growth with those of social development introduced by many of the post-colonial states in the 1950s, became the means by which the objectives of broad-based socio-economic development might be achieved. With this focus on the role of the state, the UN replaced the World Bank as the focal point for the debate on development, and many of the strategies of the Second Development Decade were incorporated in the Basic Needs and Integrated Rural Development approaches of the United Nations Development Programme (UNDP) and other specialized agencies such as the ILO, FAO and WHO.

In the meantime, the formation by Third World countries of the Group of 77 non-aligned countries (G-77) created an international political environment in which these states felt empowered and supported in their call for a New International Economic Order (NIEO), which focused on macro issues such as terms of trade and promoted more equitable relations between states as necessary for the achievement of the goals of growth with equity. The UN became the major arena for debate, and the countries of the G-77 had found their voice, a forum and a champion for their cause. In a sense, these debates of the 1970s reflected critiques of the prevailing development model, and the debates at the UN and in the North–South dialogues were paralleled by a search for 'another development' among non-governmental actors – academics and activists – in other arenas.[6]

The decade of the 1980s

However, all international debates on equity and participation came to an abrupt end with the emergence of conservative governments in the USA and Britain. The year 1980 marked a turning point. At the conference of the heads of the seven leading industrialized states (the G-7) held in Cancun that year, President Ronald Reagan of the USA and Prime Minister Margaret Thatcher of Britain formed the alliance that was to lead to the abandonment of the strategies for a Third Development Decade and their replacement with the neo-liberal agenda: a 'Washington Consensus' replaced the consensus of the 1970s on how to achieve the goals of broad-based socio-economic development. The macro-economic policy framework of structural adjustment and stabilization became the framework of development planning; the interests of international capital replaced those of people in the policy dialogues that took place between the IFIs and the governments of the South; and the International Monetary Fund replaced the UN at the heart of international policy debates. The challenges of this policy framework for women will be discussed more fully in Chapters 4 and 5.

The decade of the 1990s

The collapse of the Soviet Union in 1990, and with it the socialist alternative, further reinforced the triumph of the market over the state. The neo-liberal policy framework of the Washington Consensus came to be viewed as the only option for all countries, and the widespread adoption of a single macro-economic policy framework established the basis for the liberalization of markets, including international markets. The phrase 'there is no alternative' (TINA), attributed to Margaret Thatcher, which became the mantra of the 1980s, spread into the 1990s.

With the conclusion of the Uruguay Round of trade negotiations in 1991, and the liberalization of international trade, the World Trade Organization (WTO) became the key international institution, eclipsing the IFIs as well as the UN. In the decade of the 1990s the focus was on global markets, and trade replaced development as the central issue for countries of the South.[7]

With the collapse of the Soviet Union and the ending of the Cold War, the East–West axis was removed, focusing attention exclusively on the North–South axis, not just in geographic terms but also in class terms: as economic restructuring progressed, increasing attention was drawn to the existence of spreading pockets of poverty in the North (a 'South' in the North) and the expansion of wealth among a small group of elites in the South (a 'North' in the South). This provided a common global context for women from around the world, which helped promote solidarity among activists from different countries as they confronted the common problems created by corporate-led neo-liberal globalization.

Throughout the 1990s the UN, perhaps in an effort to regain its lost status, organized a series of conferences on global issues: a Children's Summit in New York in 1990; a UN Conference on Environment and Development (UNCED) in Rio in 1991; a Conference on Human Rights in Vienna in 1993; an International Conference on Population and Development (ICPD) in Cairo in 1994; a World Summit on Social Development in Copenhagen in 1995; and two conferences in 1996, Habitat (Istanbul) and the World Food Summit (Rome). In a sense, these conferences reflected a tacit acknowledgement, once again (as in the decade of the 1970s), of the failure of development policies and programmes to deliver on their promise of improving living conditions for the majority of the world's population.

It was in this decade, in the context of these global conferences, that the contours of a global women's movement emerged, a movement that brought a particular and different perspective to bear on problems and issues of concern of everyone. Chapter 6 will examine in detail the ways in which women organized and had an impact on these conferences. I turn now to the UN Decade for Women, the context in which women from their local origins and struggles convened to find an identity, a voice and an awareness of their power to make a difference in a world not of their making.

Background to the Decade for Women (1975–85)

Three international movements converged at the United Nations to contribute to the designation of 1975 as IWY: the women's rights movement, the human rights movement, and the movements against colonialism. As acknowledged in Chapter 2, women were, of course, actively involved in the liberation and human rights movements, but they had also formed their own independent movements within these struggles.

The UN had been a major arena for the human rights movement; indeed, the Universal Declaration on Human Rights was one of the first important instruments adopted by the world body in 1948, and Eleanor Roosevelt, by the power of her presence and strongly influenced by women from Latin America and Africa,[8] had raised issues of women's rights to a prominent place in the General Assembly.

At the same time, the strengthening of Third World membership in the UN brought an increasing number of women with backgrounds in their national liberation struggles into the UN system. Their presence was to change the tenor of the male-dominated organization.

The women's rights movement was largely an upshot of the movement for women's suffrage that blossomed in the latter part of the 19th century, and women from different countries had already formed alliances to advance their common cause.[9] The Inter-American Commission on the Status of Women (CIM), established in 1920, had been one of the groups instrumental in getting the equal rights provision into the Charter of the newly established UN; while the International Council of Women and the International Alliance of Women were among the NGOs that had consultative status with the UN Economic and Social Council (ECOSOC) and therefore membership on the UN Commission on the Status of Women (CSW), which had been established to satisfy the mandate of the Charter.

Apart from this focus on women's rights within the UN, we have seen that women around the world had been identifying their own struggles within larger processes of class struggle and national liberation. The focus on the role and status of women within the international system established for the purpose of enshrining and expanding human rights was therefore an idea whose time had come.

While the precise efforts that led to the designation of 1975 as IWY are not clear, it is certain that the UN's receptivity to the idea owed a great deal to the efforts of the women's organizations that were part of the CSW as well as to women on the delegations of member countries.[10] Since NGOs could not address the UN Assembly directly, it was the delegate from Romania, a communist country, who, at the 1972 meeting of the General Assembly, actually introduced the resolution calling for a specially designated year for women.[11] There were strong objections from the representative from Saudi Arabia who, in numerous statements before the Committee, 'argued that the conference was unnecessary, that women already had more equality than men in that they were supported by men and that when a man died his wife inherited ... [and that] such a conference would be disruptive'.[12] Princess Ashraf Pahlavi of Iran, the Shah's twin sister and chairwoman of a UN consultative committee on women, who was to be a leading supporter of the Decade, countered his argument, stating that '"male imperialism ... has paralyzed an important part of society in both developed and developing countries" and called on women to stop being "a colony of man"'.[13] The references to imperialism and colonialism were significant in the context of the time. The resolution was adopted.

Conclusion

This chapter shows the important role that the UN played in drawing attention to the issues that determined the context for women's organizing in the South, up to 1975 and beyond.

In the years ahead, the global context was increasingly one that shaped the lives of women from the North, West and East as well, so that by the 1990s, the global context was one to which all women could relate.

Notes

1 Support for a resolution calling for a UN Decade for Women came out of the UN Commission on the Status of Women and the Inter-American Commission on the Status of Women.

2 It is interesting to note that the same arguments and assumptions are being used today.

3 This included investments in ports and airports, roads, electricity, water and even factory space at peppercorn rentals.

4 Mainly exemptions on the payments of import duties and income taxes for foreign firms operating export industries.

5 This strategy was based, not on the Soviet model, but on approaches influenced by the British economist John Maynard Keynes. It was an approach that gave the state responsibility for promoting full employment and guaranteeing social services.

6 The term, 'another development', was coined in the process of debates involving academic economists and social activists focusing on the failure of development policies to improve the lives of the poor.

7 See John Madley's book in this series, *Hungry for Trade: How the Poor Pay for Free Trade*, for a full discussion of the debates on globalization and trade in the decade of the 1990s, and the impact on the poor.

8 According to Margaret Bruce, an employee in the first UN office in San Francisco when the Declaration was drafted, three women from Latin America and three from Africa worked with Eleanor Roosevelt on the drafting, and were responsible for convincing her to include the phrase 'discrimination on the basis of sex' rather than the less revolutionary 'equality among men and women', which had been her preference. This is mentioned in Suares Toto (2000), in an interview with Margaret Bruce, then in her nineties, on the occasion of the fiftieth anniversary of the Declaration.

9 At the beginning of the 20th century, the only country that allowed women to vote was New Zealand, but women in other countries had already started to organize towards the suffrage.

10 Arvonne S. Fraser (1987) describes the origins of the UN Commission for Women in the women's rights movement.

11 This strategy has played an important role in UN debates, hence the strategic importance of having representatives of NGOs as members of official delegations.

12 Arvonne Fraser (1997) gives a revealing account of this.

13 Ibid., p. 12.

4 | A Decade for Women: UN conferences, 1975–85

The appearance of a global women's movement as part of an emerging global civil society has its origins in the processes generated by the UN Decade for Women (1975–85). It was within this context that women from around the world first encountered each other in a sustained and ever-deepening process focused on their position and condition. The Decade was to nurture and expand this movement in a way that not even its strongest protagonists could have imagined.

The Decade opened spaces for women from communities all over the world to meet. They came from different racial and ethnic groups, countries, cultures, classes and occupational backgrounds, meeting on a consistent and continuous basis, from local to global levels, from the official forums of governmental conferences to the informal gatherings of women in their circles of friendship, religious, political and professional affiliations. These meetings enabled women to gain new knowledge and to learn from each other's experience. They facilitated the organization of joint projects and collaborative efforts. They gave birth to issue-based networks at local, regional and global levels, which in turn provided the research and analysis that served to empower women's advocacy. They helped women to develop self-confidence and leadership skills. They linked activists with researchers and, more importantly, validated and encouraged the pursuit of research among activists, and activism among researchers. They forged and strengthened links between organizing at local and global levels. They facilitated the growth of a global women's movement of the greatest diversity and decentralization, a movement that expanded its agenda from a narrow definition of 'women's issues' to one that embraced a range of concerns for human welfare. In the process it transformed itself into a major alternative political constituency.

The context for International Women's Year (1975)

The process leading up to the celebration of IWY was one of heightened interest in the role and status of women worldwide. At national and regional levels there were numerous research projects, as well as national, regional and international preparatory meetings. But beyond the official studies and meetings, women all over the world were responding to the new interest in their situation with a variety of initiatives, from grassroots projects to legislative initiatives. There was a sense of excitement and anticipation, even before the observance of 'The Year'.

In the USA a 'third wave' of the US women's movement had been building with the formation of the National Organization of Women (NOW) in 1966 and the Women's Equity Action League in 1968. They had been making gains in anti-discriminatory legislation.

Feminist activism around the world was reflected in the work of the women's collective, ISIS, founded in 1974 'to promote the widest possible exchange of ideas, contacts and resources among women and women's groups in Africa, Asia, Australia and Latin America and to women and women's groups in Europe and North America'. ISIS local groups, run by volunteers, were producing materials – newsletters, bulletins, films, videotapes, songs, poetry, research, books, photographs, magazines, artwork – information not readily available through the established communication channels or widely available outside local situations.[1]

Another international newsletter, *WIN NEWS*, launched in January 1975 and edited by Fran Hoskins of the USA, reflected the importance of the communications that were taking place between women around the world before the conference was held. This first publication was filled with information on the upcoming conference, along with the women's resolutions from the earlier UN 1974 population conference and the world food conference.

The publication in 1970 of Ester Boserup's trail-blazing book, *Women's Role in Economic Development*, attracted the attention of women in aid agencies in the USA and Europe, and in 1972 a group of women in Washington succeeded in introducing 'the

Personal reflection

In order to introduce the debate on the New International Economic Order into the agenda at the IWY conference, the item had to appear in one of the reports from the regional preparatory meetings. Up to the time of the final regional meeting, in Latin America, the issue had not emerged, so it was up to the women in this region to correct the omission.

I recall very well the struggle to get the paragraphs into the document at the meeting in Caracas early in 1975. As the Director of the Jamaica Women's Bureau, I was attending my first UN meeting. However, because no one in the Ministry of Foreign Affairs considered it important, I was not briefed on Jamaica's position on the various items on the agenda. In Caracas I proceeded to speak out of my own limited and uninformed understanding, and found myself frequently agreeing with the representatives of the USA rather than with those of Cuba, Mexico and Venezuela, who were obviously working to instructions from their governments to ensure that the issue would be on the agenda of the conference.

This proved controversial. Most of the participants had not yet been exposed to the research that was to link the condition of women in their countries to the larger structural issues of colonialism and neo-colonialism. When the item was discussed, some delegates, including myself, were ill prepared and found ourselves agreeing with those from the USA and Canada that the matter was irrelevant to women. It was an experience I have never forgotten, and one that I like to recount as an example of my own innocence at the outset of this Decade.

Percy Amendment' to the US Foreign Assistance Act. This highlighted the important role of women in Third World development, and required that particular attention be paid to women in development assistance programmes and projects. It was to become a model for women working in the field of foreign assistance in other developed countries, and the means for channelling resources to women's projects and programmes in developing countries.

In Third World countries, women within political parties and governments were beginning to take advantage of the heightened awareness of women's role and status to push forward their own agendas for change in the laws and practices that limited their opportunities. An example of the mood of the early 1970s was the decision by the newly elected government of Jamaica to set up an Advisory Committee on the Status of Women. Their recommendations resulted in the appointment of an Advisor on Women's Affairs and in the establishment of a Women's Desk within the machinery of government. The purpose of this 'national machinery for the integration of women in development' was to promote the full participation of women in the development of their countries, and in the benefits derived thereof.

At the UN, Helvi Sipala of Finland was appointed Secretary General of the conference. As Assistant Secretary General for Social Development and Humanitarian Affairs, she was the highest-ranking woman ever appointed to the UN up to that time. A lawyer, she came to the UN with a history of association with women's organizations in her country and internationally[2] and she represented her country on the UN Commission on the Status of Women twice, from 1960–68, and again in 1971. She was well respected at the UN and by the women who had worked for the designation of the Year. Although her task was not an easy one, she was fortunate to be operating in an international environment that was open to issues of equity in international relations. At the same time she was able to tap into the local women's movements that were emerging from the activism of the 1960s.

Eighteen background papers prepared for the conference, commissioned by UN agencies and NGOs with consultative status to the UN such as the International Planned Parenthood Federation (IPPF); were generally focused on women's role within the family. The link between women's reproductive and productive roles was explored in a study by IPPF; however the concept of 'reproductive' was biological and had not yet taken in the full range of activities that constitute social reproduction – the care and upbringing of children, household maintenance work of all types, and the socio-cultural functions involved in the reproduction of institutions such as the family.

International Women's Year (1975)

The conference marking IWY was held in Mexico City amid great anticipation. It was the first official women's conference organized by the UN and there were no guidelines, but the significance attached to it by many women could be gauged from the fact that over 8,000 women and men participated (70 per cent women) in the conference and the parallel meeting for representatives of women's organizations, *La Tribune*. At the conference, participants were drawn from 125 of the 133 UN member states, while at the tribune participants were fairly evenly distributed between those from Mexico, North America and the rest of the world.

The themes of IWY – Equality, Development and Peace – were symbolized in a stylized dove of peace, incorporating the symbols of women and equality. This was to become a powerful 'international symbol of the drive for women's equality, reprinted literally millions of times, recaptured in jewelry and printed on fabric used the world over ... put on stickers, bags, and appearing in countless publications'.[3] While participants at the conference emphasized the links between the themes, the full realization of these linkages had to await the theoretical and political work of feminist scholars and activists engaged in this project throughout the ensuing Decade.

The issues that were to frame the discussions were laid out in the opening ceremony. The two main speakers, the UN Secretary General and the President of Mexico, referred to the international debate on the NIEO and to the difference in the experiences of women from the industrialized countries of the North and those from the developing countries of the South. Mrs Sipala, the Secretary General of the conference, highlighted the commonalties between women from North and South, laying out a framework

41

for the collaborative work that would enable women from different countries and backgrounds to respect differences and forge the solidarity that would give birth to a global movement:

> Admittedly, the status of women differs significantly from country to country, due to cultural, political, economic and social factors. There are also divergences in the condition of women within countries themselves, particularly between rich and poor, rural and urban, privileged and underprivileged. But I do not see a conflict between the prevailing conditions in developing and industrialized countries as regards the real aspiration of women for social justice and a better life. In fact, women throughout the world share so many problems that they can and must support and reinforce each other in a joint effort to create a better world.[4]

The debates at the conference focused on those basic concerns of women that found support from the majority of member states, meaning that many issues that were of concern, such as violence, sexuality and sexual orientation, were absent from the discussion at this first meeting (although they were to appear in subsequent meetings as women found the confidence and power to advance them). The issues on the agenda were: literacy, education and training; health, nutrition and population; the family, household and marriage; employment and economic issues such as minimum wages, access to credit, self-employment and cooperatives; housing; political participation; international cooperation, peace and human rights; and special mechanisms for following up the recommendations of the Plan of Action. In recognition of the dearth of data on the role and status of women, special attention was paid to research. Acknowledging that a major obstacle to improving the status of women lay in public attitudes and values, the role of the mass media in influencing these was highlighted in the Plan of Action. Recommendations were addressed to the UN and other international organizations, to national governments, and an array of NGOs, from women's organizations to trades unions and political parties.

The discussions reflected both the newness of the experience for most of the delegates and the level of the research and analysis on these issues to that date. Women made up 40 per cent of the delegations, and they could be divided: those experienced in UN and other governmental meetings and those who were new to these events. At the IWY conference women were just beginning to find their public voice at an international level. The 1975 Plan of Action's silence on sexuality or sexual orientation should come as no surprise. On the other hand the absence of references to violence is interesting: it certainly could not have been that it was not an issue for women. Could it be that women participating in the regional conferences that laid the groundwork for the draft Plan of Action did not yet feel sufficiently confident to break the silence, or could it be evidence of the extent to which the agenda was ultimately controlled by men? Such an omission would be unthinkable by the end of the Decade.

The big 'political' issues for the conference were the NIEO and the linking of Zionism with racism and apartheid. Regarding the NIEO, as stated above, women were not prepared for this, and it was not well integrated into the analysis of women's concerns, although the UN Secretary General recognized the importance of a more equitable global economic and social system in facilitating the move towards equality, development and peace for women and men. Similarly, the positions taken by most Third World delegations on the Israeli–Palestinian struggle were those of their governments and did not reflect concerns that had been worked through by women. In the end, the G-77 formed their own working group to draft the more political 'Declaration of Mexico', which was adopted despite the objections of many industrialized countries.

In the geo-political climate of the mid-1970s, North–South differences were clear, and reference is often made to the distinction between a 'feminist' and a 'developing world' perspective in some reports and publications on this conference. In 1975 there was little understanding in the industrialized countries of the North of the realities of women in developing countries, although there were feminists such as Robin Morgan and Charlotte Bunch who were creating spaces for women from the South to speak for themselves.[5]

The majority of women in Mexico City for IWY – six thousand out of the eight thousand registered – were at the NGO tribune. There, there were no restrictions on the range and depth of topics discussed. The format of the tribune was itself new, having been tested for the first time at the UN conference on environment in Stockholm in 1972 and the population conference in Bucharest in 1974. However, while in Stockholm and Bucharest it was possible to contain the discussions within the framework of formal presentations and discussions, in Mexico City, although there were thirty-five formal, planned events announced by the organizers of the tribune, discussions and debates spilt over into hallways and hotel rooms around the city. The event was tapping into a social movement whose time had come. The few guidelines put in place in Stockholm and Bucharest could not contain the excitement and energy released by this historic event in Mexico City.

No formal report of the proceedings was ever published and no statements issued from the tribune, but media reports and independent studies described an experience 'operating on the "creative edge" of chaos':

> The bickering and political rhetoric was, at times, intense. Latin American women disrupted several sessions by vehemently insisting that equality for women was attainable only after economic and social changes had been made. US women wanted to have more impact on the official UN conference … A group of critical American women led a charge on the US Embassy and another group interrupted the AID Director … claiming men had no right to represent US women at the Tribune or the conference. The complaint was that the UN conference and too many at the Tribune concentrated on political issues and not on women's concerns.[6]

This distinction between 'political issues' and 'women's concerns' was frequently made in the early years of the Decade, before a critical mass of women came to understand the relationship between women's concerns and the socio-economic structural imbalances in the economies of the North and the South, and that in this sense all of women's concerns within patriarchal societies

'Confrontation is cathartic'

Women learn(ed) about each other's situation. And the groundwork was laid for understanding that development is not just an economic problem but an individual and societal problem, with political, cultural, and economic components. They learned about each other's organizations and projects, their hopes, their frustrations, their commonalities and their differences. They learned that sheer survival was a basic issue for the majority of the world's poor women. They learned that even if they shared the same religion that religion might be interpreted differently in different countries. In at least two meetings Muslim women from different countries learned that their interpretation of the Koran was not the same. And they learned that confrontation and anger are cathartic. Everyone's view was heard. American women learned that they could be the target of public vilification which shocked many of them deeply ... Americans want to be liked, and the new U.S. women's movement had taught many American women to think of all women as friends, people united in a common cause. To find that not true, in their first international encounter, was, to some, an infuriating and very disappointing experience.[7]

were indeed about structural power imbalances between men and women and therefore 'political'. While North American feminists understood that the 'personal was political', they tended to think of this in terms of individual experience.

But while the events in Mexico City tended to be misrepresented by the press in North America, the mainstream media in other parts of the world largely ignored them.

Mexico City 1975 may not have been the earth-shattering event anticipated by many, but it was the beginning of a process that was indeed to change the lives of many women, the first step towards the realization of the prediction made in the introduction to the World Plan of Action for Women that emerged from the conference, 'In our times, women's role will emerge as a powerful, revolutionary social force'.

The Decade for Women (1975–85)

The first five years Even before the conference, it was clear that one year was not going to be enough for women finally getting a chance to present their concerns to the international community. The Decade for Women (1975–85) was recommended by the conference and later that year adopted by the UN General Assembly. The designation of a Decade was crucial for the building and nurturing of an international movement. Indeed, it is doubtful if such a movement could have emerged without the resources, opportunities and events made possible by this Decade.

Building on the momentum created by IWY, women everywhere lost no time in pursuing the goals and objectives of the Plan of Action. Special mechanisms ('national machinery' – women's commissions, bureaux, desks, units) were established within government bureaucracies as well as within international institutions and bilateral assistance programmes; new women's organizations were formed and old ones re-energized; women's studies programmes were established in many universities around the world; researchers within and outside academia, research institutes and government agencies worked to fill the data gap and new research institutes focusing on women were formed in many countries.

An International Women's Tribune Centre (IWTC) was established in New York City, across the street from the UN. According to its founder, Anne Walker, who had organized the tribune in Mexico, IWTC was set up to respond to the needs of the women who had participated in the Mexico City events. Coming out of Mexico City there was a mailing list of thousands, material from the tribune and conference and clear indications that this was just the beginning of something new and meaningful to countless women from across the globe. It was IWTC that introduced many of the new networks of women in developing countries to the computer technology that was to prove a powerful tool in the transformation of communications between women worldwide.

The focus: integrating Women in Development (WID) Women in Development (WID) programmes and projects in many developing countries grounded the work of women's organizations in issues of concern to women in their everyday lives, and contributed to strengthening and expanding women's organizing at local levels. Indeed, the line between the bureaucratized work on WID, women's groups and organizations, and an emerging social movement focused on the condition and position of women, was often blurred. Irene Tinker, one of the pioneers in the field of WID, describes the field as being defined by three categories of women – scholars, advocates and practitioners – but the designations often overlapped, especially for the activist.

The role of the activist/scholar, grounded in feminist theory, was crucial in this process of transforming the work of traditional women's organizations and bureaucratic initiatives into part of a political movement. In the first five years, this process manifested itself in the work of feminist scholars with Marxist or socialist orientation. They started by challenging the assumptions underlying the WID thesis.

The focus on the 'integration of women in development' was inspired by Ester Boserup's 1969 study on the 'invisibility' of women's contribution to development. There she had argued that women had been marginalized from the development process both absolutely (by being displaced from their traditional roles and activities) and relatively (by not being taken into account explicitly in development efforts and not enjoying the presumed gains from development on equal terms with men). The WID approach fitted into the dominant development paradigm of the time – modernization theory – and at the official level of WID programmes no one challenged this, least of all people working with the national machineries and special units established within various institutions to implement the Plan of Action adopted at the 1975 Conference.

Feminists challenging the paradigm From the very beginning, how-ever, Third World women were to challenge this paradigm. They argued that women were already 'integrated' into a development process that subjected them to subordination and exploitation, and they asked questions about the kind of development that would meet women's concerns.[8] They criticized Boserup for not challenging the modernization paradigm and for assuming that the capitalist model of development was benign. They also argued that the exploitation of women's time and labour was central to capitalist development, pointing out the usefulness of women's subsistence production to the process of capitalist accumulation. According to many of them:

> The problem of women's subordination required a more funda-mental change in the development process, one that tackled the inequities in the global economic system and focused on changing exploitative class relations as well as women's subordination.[9]

Following a meeting held at Wesley College in the USA in 1976, African women took the first steps to challenge Western hegemony in the field of research on Third World women,[10] forming the African Association for Women and Development (AAWORD). Other Third World women were to follow in this path, establishing their own research programmes which inevit-ably gave rise to alternative analyses and ways of looking at the reality of women.

A workshop on 'Feminist ideologies and structures in the first half of the Decade', sponsored by the UN Asia & Pacific Centre for Women and Development (APCWD) and held in Bangkok in 1979, brought home the relevance of feminism[11] to many of the Third World women present. Because of its analysis of power, from the personal to the political, and by relating this to women's experience in other liberation struggles, such as the civil rights and independence movements, some women made the connec-tion between the marginalization and structured powerlessness of women and other movements that attempted to address issues of structural imbalance between people and countries, including the call for a NIEO. The workshop was an example of the kind of questioning that was taking place among women working within bureaucratic settings such as national machinery and the UN itself, and an indication of the power of feminism to transform the thinking of women for whom, initially, it had been alienating. It was good preparation for the mid-decade conference scheduled to take place in Copenhagen the following year.

Mid-Decade (1980)

By the time of the 1980 conference and NGO Forum (the equivalent of the tribune in Mexico City) the number of women catalysed by the 1975 events had grown to such an extent that it was no surprise that numbers in Copenhagen exceeded those in Mexico City. But the conference and Forum were not only much larger in size (about 2,000 at the conference and 8,000 at the Forum), but inevitably imbued with greater realism than the events five years earlier. By this time, the statistics that were to become a mantra for bureaucrats and activists worldwide had been widely disseminated, as the UN said, 'Women, constituting fifty percent of the world's population, carry out two-thirds of the world's work and earn one tenth of the world's income.'

The research and analysis of the four years since 1975 gave women a much clearer understanding of the issues; their experience in projects and programmes, advocacy and policy-making generated a level of confidence that better prepared them for the mid-Decade events; and networking ensured that women had begun to work together across national boundaries and from local to global levels. All of this translated into a conference and Forum that were much more contentious and at the same time more reflective of the reality of the lives of the women of a world divided by huge imbalances in political and economic power.

The mid-Decade conference The Secretary General for this conference was Lucille Mair of Jamaica,[12] whose style and political savvy reflected the emerging leadership of women from the South. The conference was intended as an opportunity to readjust programmes for the second half of the Decade in light of new data and research, and focused on the sub-themes of education,

49

employment and health; but Lucille's leadership placed these issues in a much more political context. The data revealed the complexity of women's condition within a patriarchal world, and while the word 'patriarchy' was taboo in the conference debates, it was clear that attitudes, customs and laws that entrenched male power and privilege were not going to be easily changed.

The conference broke new ground by discussing the root causes of women's inequality. This was seen as the result of historical processes – economic, social, political and cultural – that produced a sexual division of labour based on women's childbearing function; this was used to justify confining women to the domestic domain of the household. But there was also an acknowledgement of the ways in which unjust economic structures – capitalism, colonialism and neo-colonialism – had generated and exacerbated the poverty in which the majority of women in developing countries lived.

Discussions on women's inequality revealed the tension between advocacy for women's equality and the fear that women's advancement through socio-economic development and legislative change would erode 'cultural values', a code word for male privilege. For the first time domestic and sexual violence were discussed, along with the issue of female circumcision. These were not new issues for women, but their appearance on the agenda of a conference sponsored by a male-dominated institution was as much a tribute to the tenacity of women within the UN system and the female delegates who had political clout in their own countries as it was to the men who aligned themselves with women in these difficult discussions.

The issues that dominated the conference were those related to the Israeli–Palestinian conflict, the plight of refugee and displaced women, and apartheid. Many delegates accepted the media's characterization of the conference as being too 'political'.[13] The presence in Copenhagen of the Palestinian hijacker, Leila Khaled, who spoke out against Israel in many workshops at the NGO Forum, did nothing to help the public image of the event.

However, to characterize issues of apartheid, the Palestinian–Israeli conflict and the plight of refugees and displaced persons

– issues of deep concern to African and Palestinian women – as 'political' was to have a narrow interpretation of the word. Equality for women is a deeply political issue, and especially in many of the countries of Africa, Asia and Latin America. So are issues of employment, education and health for poor people, since they relate to the allocation of economic resources within an economic framework geared to the exclusion of large sectors of the population. However, the majority of women in both the conference and Forum were probably not yet clear on this matter.

In the event, women on the delegations from the industrialized countries were no more able to tackle these issues than were the women from developing countries.[14] In fact, when these issues were being discussed at the conference, it was the male members of all delegations who took the seats reserved for those who would engage in the debate. By the time of the end-of-Decade conference in Nairobi, there was less of this ludicrous exchange of chairs. Women were sufficiently familiar with the rules and issues to be entrusted by their governments to carry the debate. The price was the muting of any discussion that might have brought new perspectives or broken new ground. This had to await the clearer articulation of feminist analyses on social, economic, political and cultural issues by feminists from NGOs who were able to get on to the delegations in the conferences of the 1990s, and at the Fourth World Conference on Women in 1995.

Another shift that could be noted in conference proceedings was the clearer articulation of the role of women's organizations and grassroots organizations. In Mexico City emphasis had been on the role of governments: to set up special mechanisms, to change laws, to provide services for the most marginalized women. In Copenhagen, the role of women's organizations in generating political will was recognized, as well as their role in promoting self-reliance. The references to the need for self-reliance could also be read as foreshadowing the withdrawal of the state from responsibility for basic services, a shift that was to characterize state policies in many countries in the decade of the 1980s. However, once again, this was not yet an issue for women, and the recognition of their need to break dependency and their capacity for self-reliance was viewed as a step in the right direction.

The Forum The theme of the Forum could have been 'sharing experience of the first five years'. As a result of recommendations in the Plan of Action, European and North American foreign aid agencies[15] and foundations had been supporting women's programmes and projects in developing countries, and these agencies funded many of the participants at the Forum. The Forum provided a unique opportunity for women who had been involved in these programmes and projects to talk about their work and achievements to women from other countries.

There were workshops on every topic. A series of workshops, *The Exchange*,[16] typified these activities. One of its workshops on 'feminism' used a videotape, 'World Feminists', as the basis for small group discussions.[17] The focus of these discussions changed according to the different emphases and interests of the particular group of participants. The experience showed both that feminism was widespread and that it was not homogeneous, since it represented the struggles of women from different locations and with different concerns and priorities.

In the open space created by the Forum organizers, workshops ranged from one on 'Women's exploitation by transnational corporations', organized by the World Peace Council, to workshops on infant feeding practices. Newly established women's studies programmes met to share research findings and experience, and explored the possibilities for establishing an international association of women's studies.[18]

The workshops provided the space for women working on common agendas to meet, share experiences and strategize for the future. Networks were formed and many women left the Forum, and the conference, recognizing the need for a different approach to their work, and aware of the enormity of the task ahead.

The second half of the Decade

The mid-Decade conference and Forum had not only increased the number of women working on the plans and programmes of action, but also changed the way in which many worked. There was a greater awareness of the impact of political and economic factors on women's lives. Many women had learned for the first time about the crisis in the Middle East, and were beginning to learn about the impact of the looming debt crisis. Above all, with the swing to conservative governments in the USA and Britain, women were about to understand the need to pay attention to the policy framework that was to have such an impact on the lives of women, especially poor women. Chapter 4 will focus on the Decade of the 1980s that was to have such significance for the strengthening of the movement.

The Nairobi conference The preparations, official and informal, for the end of Decade conference and Forum were filled with excitement and anticipation. In the first instance, it was going to be a gathering of women who had got to know each other well through the many meetings that had taken place over the ten years since 1975; they had worked together; learned about the world and about the UN and about each other's lives. They did not always agree in their politics or analysis, but they had learned to respect each other.

The location of Nairobi for the final conference and Forum of the Decade gave these events special significance. As the Decade progressed, women from the economic South had become increasingly visible in the leadership of the movement at the international level; the meetings in Nairobi provided these women with an opportunity to show that leadership. Third World women had finally come into their own in the international community and, with this greater sense of their own identity, were now ready to redefine the notion of 'global sisterhood' into global solidarity among women. While the North–South divide did not disappear, there was a new confidence among women from the South that facilitated the creation of a partnership between them in the struggle for a better world.

As in the previous events, the leadership went to women who were well known internationally and experienced in international negotiations. Letitia Shahani of the Philippines was Secretary

General for the conference, while Nita Barrow of Barbados was Convener for the Forum.

The mandate for the conference was to produce 'forward-looking strategies'. The final conference of the Decade would be an appraisal of the progress made and the obstacles to the implementation of the recommendations from the conferences in Mexico City and Copenhagen, with a focus on the strategies that would take these forward. Because of the activism of women's movements around the world during the Decade, along with the commitment of women (and men) working in the bureaucracies of states and international agencies to implement the agendas produced by the earlier conferences, governments were certainly more aware of what women wanted. Most governments responded to the questionnaires that formed the basis for assessment of the progress and obstacles in advancing the status of women, and the official reports would have given the most favourable impressions of progress at national level. However, the truth is that, despite tremendous efforts and the resources provided by governments, foundations and other donors, women's condition continued to deteriorate during the Decade. How could it be otherwise, when the Decade took place during a period marked by major setbacks in the economies of many of the countries! Although this was acknowledged in the 'Historical Background to the Forward Looking Strategies', as well as in the 'Obstacles to Development', there was nothing in the strategies themselves that addressed these issues.

An analysis of the conference documents and recommendations reveals the importance of the international political context in which these conferences take place. While the discussions on the obstacles to women's advancement in the area of male attitudes were much stronger than they had been ten years earlier in Mexico City, those related to the policy framework, and the international environment that would enable the implementation of programmes that were fundamental to women's advancement, were not. The discussion on the importance of a NIEO for the generation of resources that would finance essential programmes in the areas of women's health and education in developing countries, which dominated the agenda in 1975, was referred to in vague terms in the section on 'Current Trends and Perspectives to the Year 2000'. The change in the political context since 1980 was reflected in the conference. UN conferences reflect the relative strengths of the various blocs within that organization, and the prevailing priorities of member states: the ascendancy of conservative governments in the North, together with the weakened position of the developing countries in the context of the spreading debt crisis, not to mention their adoption of the policy framework of structural adjustment, would certainly be major obstacles to the implementation of the Programme of Action from Copenhagen, as well as the strategies adopted at the conference.

Nevertheless, the conference did mark a significant advance over the others in terms of the number of women among the delegations (women outnumbered men), their experience, level of awareness of the complexity of the obstacles to women's advancement, and their willingness to tackle issues that had not been dealt with in the earlier conferences. These issues included violence against women and the abuse of women and children, women's access to legal redress, and pornography. In the section on Equality there was a reference to 'deeply rooted resistance on the part of conservative elements in society to the change in attitudes necessary for a total ban on discriminatory practices against women at the family, local, national and international levels' (paragraph 50). However, the conference stopped short of identifying religious fundamentalism as one of these conservative elements.

On the other hand, there were short sections on 'Women and Children under Apartheid' and 'Palestinian Women and Children', with clear calls for support for the women's sections of national liberation movements, the eradication of apartheid and the 'rights of Palestinian people to the recovery of their rights to self-determination and the right to establish an independent state in accordance with all relevant UN resolutions' (paragraph 306). As in the case of the Copenhagen conference, there was also a clearer understanding of the importance of the role of women's organizations in securing the political will for change.

Nevertheless, the 'strategies' continued to sidestep the question of what has come to be termed the 'enabling international economic environment'. Silence on this issue was perhaps to be expected, given the fact that this conference took place at a time when most governments were not yet ready to challenge the Washington Consensus. The fact that the critiques of these policies were being discussed at the NGO Forum is an indication of the differences between these two spaces. UN conferences are inter-governmental events, where the interests of governments, rather than those of women, determine the scope of debate.

The Forum Forum '85 was better planned than any of the preceding events, not only by the organizers, but also by women's organizations throughout the world. Under the inspiring leadership of Nita Barrow, Third World women saw this as their special event and mobilized to make it a memorable one. They also took responsibility for ensuring that this Forum would reflect their perspectives. Thus African women met in two preparatory conferences, one for Kenyan women, the other a regional meeting held in Arusha. The report from the Arusha conference highlighted the inadequacies of policies and programmes that left the situation of the majority of women unchanged, despite the gains that were made. The report highlighted the obstacles to women's advancement stemming from male domination as well as from the negative teachings of many of the world religions.

In Bangalore, India, a small meeting was convened to prepare a platform document for the Forum. *Development, Crises and Alternative Visions*, prepared by DAWN, offered a critique of the growth-oriented economic model that had contributed to the perpetuation of women's poverty and marginalization.[19]

The quality of these preparatory meetings was reflected in the numbers of women attracted to the Forum, as well as in the quality of participation. Although the organizers of the forum expected the numbers to exceed those attending the event in 1980, nothing prepared them for what actually transpired. One commentator, in summing up the difference between the 1975 event and this one, put it this way:

56

In the intervening decade a critical mass of women had moved from detailing their oppression to understanding their power through organizational efforts.[20]

It was the largest gathering of women from around the world to that date: 13,504 registered, but this does not represent the total number of participants in what has been described as 'a cross between an international fair and a university symposium'.[21] Secondly, perhaps because of its location on the African continent, Third World women predominated (60 per cent of the total, with more than a thousand from Kenya alone). More importantly, while feminism had been marginalized in Mexico and to a lesser extent in Copenhagen, here in Nairobi it was central to the organizing, highlighting the fact that feminism, grounded in an analysis of the structured relationships of power between men and women, could also help women understand other structured relationships of power between other groups – rich and poor, black and white – and even countries. Feminism was seen as a politics as relevant to Third World women as it was to women from North America and Europe.

FORUM HIGHLIGHTS Some of the most compelling events were explicitly feminist, including the series of panels organized by the DAWN group, based on the platform document prepared at the Bangalore meeting. More importantly, by showing how neo-colonial relations and macro-economic policy affected women's lives, DAWN introduced an analytical framework which was to change the terms of the debate on women's issues.

Another breakthrough was the diversity of the women gathered in Nairobi: diversity in class, race and political orientation was clearer in this event than in any of the others.

Finally, the political sophistication of participants might be gauged from the fact that, by this time, it was understood that the time to influence the conference documents was in the capitals, and that only minor changes could be effected during the event itself. The decision to hold the Forum before the conference was intended to allow conference participants opportunities to benefit from discussions at the Forum, and Forum participants opportunities to participate in the conference.

Another highlight of Forum '85 was the Peace Tent, a space in which sharp political differences could be negotiated. There, women from Palestine and Israel, Iran and Iraq, America and the Soviet Union, met for dialogues that did not necessarily lead to agreement but to a deeper understanding of the divisions between them. The sign outside the Tent read: 'Respect for another's experience and views, openness and a spirit of cooperation, finding common ground for action in a diversity of opinions'.

THE FINAL REPORT The final report of the forum, *For the Record ... Forum '85,* summarized the meaning of the event to women as follows:

> Today women see themselves as a force for change, not just for women but for the whole of society. Women seek the power and the strength to work equally with men to change the social, political and economic structure in the direction of integral and equitable development.
>
> Since participants expressed little hope for the ability or willingness of present governments to help realize women's alternative visions, they repeatedly stressed the need for women to organize independently for political action to assume responsibility ... to challenge existing policies and programmes and to work to bring about an integral development.
>
> Central to a feminist alternative vision is a people-centred international order concerned about the poorest and most oppressed ... Stress is also placed on the importance of understanding class, race, ethnic, gender and age hierarchies as essential factors in the analyses and design of strategies not only in relation to society as a whole, but among women themselves.

This summary reflects the greater realism of the analysis along with a new emphasis on women's leadership for change – the shift from the 'integration' of women in development to 'empowering' women for social change.

Significance of the Decade for the global women's movement

The relationship between women/gender and development programmes and the global women's movement One of the significant outcomes of the UN Decade for Women was the linking of the political work of activists to the professional and technical work of practitioners and policy-makers in the field of socio-economic development. Crosscutting these two spaces – the world of practitioners and that of the activist/advocate – is the work of the researcher/academic, often women who worked in both spaces and contributed to both.

While this link between bureaucratic and policy concerns about women, and women's movements (made up of activists/advocates), has drawn criticism from feminist activists,[22] there is no doubt that, despite setbacks and limitations, the state's focus on the contribution of and benefits to women in the process of socio-economic development led to some significant gains for women.[23] Indeed, the relationship between practitioners and policy-makers in the field of women/gender and development, and women's movements' activists/advocates and researchers, has been mutually beneficial. The practitioners owe the movement the research and advocacy that have made their work more effective; the movement owes the practitioners and policy-makers the spaces and resources that have supported their work.

Specifically, practitioners in the field of women/gender and development owe to the women's movement an understanding of the political nature of development and of the theoretical underpinnings and implications of their work. Following the first intellectual efforts to make women's work visible came the questioning of the dominant paradigm of development, the ways in which it ignored or marginalized the contribution of women to socio-economic development. Later work showed that, far from being marginal to socio-economic development, the neo-classical model of development actually depended on the exploitation of women's time, labour and sexuality. At a theoretical level, feminists' focus on the study of gender as a way of understanding the social relations and perceived differences between the sexes gave practitioners the analytical tools to make their projects and programmes more effective.

The political work of the movement is different from the technical and professional work of practitioners, and just as important to the achievement of the goals of gender equality and equity. In my view, a clearer recognition of the differences between the political women's movement and the bureaucratic field of women/gender and development would allow for an appreciation of the strengths and weaknesses, the opportunities and limitations of the two spaces, and facilitate the development of strategic working relationships and more rewarding synergies between the two that would contribute to the achievement of common aims.

The role of feminist politics In speaking of the 'political' women's movement I want to be clear that I mean the feminist-led women's movement. Indeed, I believe that it is feminism that creates the link between the practitioners and policy-makers, the researchers and the activist/advocates. Feminism also makes a fundamental contribution to the field of social change (of which socio-economic development is one aspect):

- It enables one to *see the world differently*. By identifying, as a woman, with the structured marginalization, powerlessness and alienation of other marginalized groups, feminism provides a window for experiential learning. By asking different questions, feminism enables one to make connections between gender subordination and many of the problems facing the world – violence, poverty, social exclusion.
- Feminist politics provides a basis for *organizing for change* towards a vision of the world that is equitable, democratic, safe and sustainable.

The field of women and development also owes to feminist politics many of its successes. Feminist politics, facilitated by the processes of the UN Decade for Women as well as the other UN conferences, linked the work of women/gender and development to a social movement for the transformation of social relations.

Feminist leadership within the ranks of UN personnel and government delegations, as well as in the women's organizations that participated in these events, was central in building a global women's movement that incorporated and supported the work of women and development practitioners, as well as scholars and advocates.

By bringing together practitioners in the field of women and development, policy-makers, researchers, representatives of women's and feminist organizations, and women who considered themselves part of a women's movement, the UN Decade for Women, more than any other process, contributed to the building of a global women's movement of the greatest diversity imaginable.[24] Within these processes, women who might not easily have met and worked together in their own countries came to understand each other, and to discover that what they had in common was more important than what divided them. The interaction was not always easy: women from different races, ethnic groups, countries, cultures, political philosophies, ages and backgrounds had to overcome prejudices, misrepresentation and misunderstanding to work together in mutual respect.

The UN also provided the movement both with space for the formulation of programmes of action that reflected the women's demands – practical and strategic – and with international standards and instruments for achieving these. Most importantly, UN conferences provided a space where the women's movement could interact with and challenge governments to sign on to pledges, declarations and resolutions that would change the condition and position of women.

It is possible to work within a women's movement without engagement with the institutions which determine the laws and policies and allocate resources that affect the quality of our lives as women. However, the implementation of the agendas of women's movements relies on the generation of political will and bureaucratic responses. For this to happen, significant sections[25] of the women's movement must engage with mainstream political realities.

Of course there are risks. Many writers have referred to the bureaucratization of the movement. In a sense the movement itself became a victim of its successful advocacy. With the implementation of recommendations and resolutions, many activists are drawn into working relationships with women and men within the institutions and bureaucracies, and in this process have often faced accusations of being co-opted, or having sold out the movement. Those in the movement who feel this way need to consider the alternative: neglecting the opportunities for the achievement of some of the critical goals of the movement. The women's movement too must therefore come to terms with their relationship to the field of development, building strategic alliances with women on the inside of mainstream politics and bureaucracies. Here again, feminism can be a touchstone to trust.

However this is debated, there can be little doubt that WID practitioners and policy-makers from the Third World helped ground the mainstream (eurocentric) women's movement in the realities of the lives of women from different countries and cultures, and in the process broadened the movement's agenda from a narrow definition of women's issues to women's perspectives on a range of human issues.

Conclusion

The quantity and quality of the activities and commitment generated by the UN Decade for Women was unlike that of any other UN Decade. This was because, more than any other similar event, the opportunities and resources provided within the framework of the Decade for Women nurtured a social movement which was to address every aspect of life – from the personal to the political, from the domestic to the public, from the deepest levels of women's consciousness to the most outward expressions of women's agency. The feminist assertion that the personal is political reflected a position that was to challenge dichotomies in many spheres and at many levels.

In a wider sense, however, it was the achievement of many of the short-term goals of the Decade that revealed its limitations: for despite changing laws, the establishment of policies and programmes, special mechanisms and projects for ensuring the increased participation of women in development activities, the situation of women continued to deteriorate, both in terms of a widening gap between rich and poor within and between countries, and in terms of the incidence of violence against women.

By the end of the Decade, the themes of equality, development and peace had merged, and the women who had been involved in activities within this framework – research and advocacy, project implementation and policy formulation, institution building and legislative change – had moved beyond a narrow definition of women's issues to advance women's perspectives on a range of global issues within the global conferences of the 1990s: Macro-economic Policy, Environment, Human Rights, Population, Poverty, Employment, Habitats, Food and Trade.

Postscript to the Decade: the Fourth World Conference on Women (1995)

One of the recommendations from the Nairobi conference was that the UN should hold another world conference on women in ten years, to take stock of the implementation of the Platform of Action formulated in Nairobi. This conference took place in Beijing in 1995, and once again demonstrated the exponential growth of the movement, not only in numbers but in intellectual achievements, skills in organizing and negotiating, and in the sheer enthusiasm with which women prepared for and participated in this event. The conference and NGO Forum were celebrations of the global women's movement. They provided an opportunity for the women of the world to bring together the results of their rich experience of activism shaped in the global conferences of the first half of the 1990s. It was, in a sense, a showcase for the international women's movement, revealing its concerns and passions, its strategies and initiatives, its successes and failures, its strengths and limitations.

Official recognition of women's movements as important political actors, and women as an important constituency, can be gauged by the fact that the conference was addressed by the head of the World Bank, and by a representative of the

Pope (although this was not a surprise, given the fact that the Vatican had long recognized the political significance of women's movements).

In the fifteen years between the Nairobi and Beijing conferences the international women's movement had been transformed into a global women's movement through participation in the global conferences of the decade of the 1990s. The issue of women's human rights served as an overarching theme for the NGO Forum and UN conference, placing a wide range of concerns within a framework which, with its conventions and provision for legislative action, had the potential for facilitating accountability.

Notes

1 *ISIS International Bulletin*, 2 (1976).

2 In 1953 she was president of the International Federation of Women Lawyers.

3 Fraser (1987) p. 14.

4 *Meeting in Mexico*, Mimeo, 1975, UN, pp. 10–11.

5 For example, Robin Morgan's book *Sisterhood is Global* comprised statements from women from around the world, while women such as Charlotte Bunch ('Bringing the Global Home: Feminism in the '80s' in *Passionate Politics: Essays 1968–1986, Feminist Theory in Action*) were calling attention to global issues.

6 Arvonne Fraser (1987) quotes articles from the *New York Times* of 22 and 23 June 1975.

7 Fraser (1997), p. 38.

8 At the beginning of the Decade, within the framework of civil society calls for 'another development', a meeting in Scandinavia called for Another Development with Women.

9 Deere and Leal: p. 6.

10 AAWORD was launched in 1987, following a meeting of researchers working on African women held at Wesley University. Confronted by the definition of their reality by US researchers, the African women participating in the meeting decided to form their own research network.

11 I was one of the participants for whom the workshop represented a turning point. Prior to the workshop I, along with many Third World women, had difficulty identifying with feminism. Fol-

lowing the workshop I used the word as often as I could, always defining it as a 'consciousness of all the sources of women's oppression
and a commitment to challenge and change them'.

12 The person whom I had succeeded as Advisor on Women's
Affairs to the government of Jamaica, and who introduced me to this
work.

13 Mainstream media, overwhelmingly North American and
European, tend to characterize anything outside a narrow definition
of 'women's issues' as 'political', thus distorting the concerns of the
majority of women.

14 Among the exceptions were Marilyn Waring, the parliamen-
tarian from New Zealand. A feminist scholar and activist, her inter-
ventions set her apart from most other delegates.

15 In 1979, WID officers in these agencies had formed their own
informal network through the Organization for Economic Cooperation and Development's Development Assistance Committee
(OECD/DAC).

16 I worked with Kristin Anderson of the Carnegie Corporation
in the organization of these workshops on some common projects of
the first half of the Decade – national machinery, appropriate technology and income-generating projects.

17 Following my 'conversion' to feminism at the APCWD Workshop, I worked with Charlotte Bunch to contract video producer,
Martha Stewart, to produce a video that would stimulate discussion
on feminism among women from different countries and cultures.

18 Such an association was the vision of Miriam Chamberlain of
the Ford Foundation and Florence Howe of the Feminist Press.

19 The DAWN network will be discussed in greater detail in the
next chapter.

20 Arvonne S. Fraser (1987), p. 119.

21. Ibid., p. 118.

22 See Nighat Said Khan's chapter, 'The Impact of the Global
Women's Movement on International Relations: Has It Happened,
What Has Happened?' (pp. 35–45) in Braig and Wolte (2002).

23 Claudia von Braunmuhl's chapter 'Mainstreaming Gender
– a Critical Revision' (pp. 54–79) in the same book provides a good
discussion on this issue.

24 Many delegates on government delegations represented
women's organizations; many were feminists.

25 Effective political work requires multiple strategies: thus the
movement must include both the radical groups who choose to

remain adamantly on the outside, as well as those who are prepared for critical engagement with mainstream institutions. Identity politics facilitates this inside-outside strategy. This will be discussed more fully in Chapters 7 and 9.

5 | The Lost Decade – the 1980s

The decade of the 1980s warrants a special chapter because it was during this period that women came to understand the ways in which the exploitation of their time, labour and sexuality was the foundation of an economic model that was fundamentally inequitable and unjust. During this period, the spread of the policy framework of neo-liberalism, embodied in the so-called Washington Consensus through the mechanism of the condi-tionalities attached to IMF and World Bank loans to indebted countries, exposed the gender ideology underlying capitalism in ways that had not been as clear before. This policy framework

---

Personal reflection

In preparation for the events to mark the mid-point of the Decade, I was invited by the Society for International Development (SID) to prepare a document on the theme of 'Development' for the NGO Forum that was to parallel the UN conference. What I found, to my great surprise, and to the disbelief of the NGO community, was that women were actually worse off on every indicator – income, employment, health and education – than they had been in 1975. What was not recognized at the time was that this was a reflec-tion of the socio-economic deterioration being experienced in many developing countries as a result of a combination of factors: the collapse in commodity prices; recession and protectionism in the industrialized countries; the beginnings of the debt crisis; and the IMF-inspired policies of structural adjustment that were adopted as conditionalities of the IMF loans provided for its solution.

---

demonstrated, as nothing else had done before, the gender and class biases inherent in an economic model that focused on economic growth while apparently ignoring social, cultural and political factors. An understanding of the gendered nature of these policies and their impact on the poor, especially on women and on those for whom they cared – children, the elderly, the sick and disabled – served to radicalize large sections of women's movements worldwide.

A clear understanding of the macro-economic policy framework of structural adjustment is also important for understanding today's political economy of globalization, as well as the new stage of political hegemony (neo-liberalism as US imperialism) ushered in by the US-led war against Iraq. The widespread introduction of the policy framework of structural adjustment and neo-liberalism through the efforts of the IFIs, under the influence of the US Treasury, prepared the ground for trade liberalization, which required the adoption of a common policy framework by all countries. The collapse of the Soviet Union and Soviet bloc in 1989 and the absence of an alternative to capitalism reinforced this trend and the phrase 'there is no alternative' (TINA) became the mantra against which feminist activists could mobilize in the 1990s.

The macro-economic policy framework of Structural Adjustment Programmes (SAPs)

The policy package that came to be known as structural adjustment included persuading the governments of LDCs (Less Developed Countries) to cut allocations to key sectors such as education, health, welfare and agriculture; to cut subsidies to the poor; to privatize public services and public sector investments; and to devalue their currencies. Theoretically this policy package was intended to enable governments to save money so that they could service their international debt while at the same time encouraging increased production by the private sector, especially production that would earn the foreign exchange required for debt servicing.

Although it was a package designed for indebted countries, it became the policy framework for all countries wishing to 'modernize',[1] even those without a debt crisis. In this process, the International Monetary Fund replaced the UN as the international institution that framed the debates on development.[2]

But these policies were more than merely economic.[3] Their social, political and even cultural impacts were to have even more far-reaching consequences for the well-being of people than their economic impacts. By abandoning the imperatives of social development (social reproduction) in favour of those of economic growth (economic production), this policy framework undermined the very basis for economic production and productivity, since productivity is, after all, not merely a function of capital, technology and markets, but of the physical, psychological and intellectual capacities of the labour force – all of which are outcomes of social development and shaped in the domain of social reproduction.

More importantly, these policies undermined the capacity of states to guarantee the well-being of the majority of their citizens. The retreat of the state from the provision of social services and from policies to protect the most vulnerable groups compromised the very legitimacy of many states.

Above all, these policies must be seen as expressions of the Washington Consensus, the dogma of neo-liberalism. All institutions were encouraged (or obliged) to subscribe to this imposed 'consensus', and the macro-economic policy framework that it embodied was used as a conditionality in negotiations by other international and regional institutions such as the World Bank and the regional development banks, as well as in bilateral and regional aid.

Consequences of the policy framework of adjustment

As stated above, the new policy framework had economic, political, social and cultural consequences.

Economic consequences In economic terms it represented a switch from earlier emphases on Integrated Rural Development, Basic Needs and Import-Substitution-Industrialization (ISI) that were hallmarks of international thinking on 'development' in the 1960s and 1970s, to an emphasis on macro-economic planning (aimed at the reduction of fiscal deficits), the promotion of export-oriented industrial and agricultural production, and the attraction of direct foreign investments. Thus, the maintenance of roads, schools, rural clinics and extension services was sacrificed to the need to generate budget surpluses on recurrent expenditures; the needs of small farmers were neglected in favour of production of a single export crop; and the promotion and support of local entrepreneurship was set aside in favour of policies geared to attracting large-scale foreign investment.

Social consequences The social consequences received a great deal of publicity through the publication of UNICEF's groundbreaking book, *Adjustment with a Human Face* (1978). The publication, based on case studies from a number of countries, showed how these policies, through the cuts in resource allocations to social services, had a devastating effect on vulnerable groups (defined as women, children and the elderly). However, given women's role in the care of children and the elderly, it was hardly fair or accurate to link women's experience to that of children and the elderly. Feminists took this analysis further by considering the specific, gender-based, impacts of the policies on women. They showed how it was women, especially poor women, who bore the brunt of the burdens imposed by policies that privileged economic growth over human development and reduced the role of the state in guaranteeing basic needs and redistributive justice by cutting social services and subsidies for the poor – while giving advantages to the rich through the sale of assets (privatization) and tax concessions for the promotion of exports.

Political consequences The political are perhaps the most fundamental. The neo-liberal policies of the Washington Consensus signified the restructuring both of the role of the state and the relationships between states, markets and civil society. In accepting IMF conditionalities, states gave up their power to formulate policies that were in the interest of the majority of their populations. Many post-colonial states (like those of the English-speaking Caribbean) had made the establishment of the social and physical infrastructure for development a priority. The provision of basic services such as education, health, water and sanitation, electricity, transportation and personal security, were viewed as fundamental to the development of the human and physical capital essential to economic growth. A social contract, formal or informal, between the state and the market, acknowledged the state's responsibilities for guaranteeing these basic rights, including the right of workers to organize. Under the Washington Consensus this was abandoned, and replaced by a new 'contract' that favoured the interests of the market over those of civil society. People-friendly states became market-friendly states. To the extent that women look to the state to guarantee basic services, they stood to lose the most from this switch.

Cultural consequences The cultural consequences of this retreat of the state from guaranteeing the public good were even more devastating for women. Economic restructuring in the cause of global capitalism has three consequences that lead to the spread of religious fundamentalism: first, economic decline and insecurity cause people to seek the solace and certainty offered by religious fundamentalism; second, loss of access to jobs and essential services can push marginalized people to seek the assistance offered by religious groups. These groups can take advantage of the vulnerability of the poor and marginalized to indoctrinate them in the most extreme expressions of the faith they promote. This was the case with the educational and health services provided by Christian fundamentalists in Latin America in the 1980s, as it was in the case of similar services provided by Muslim fundamentalists in the Middle East and parts of Asia throughout the 1990s. Third, the threatened erosion of cultural values through the spread of Western materialism and consumerism has led many to a form of identity politics as a form of resistance to Westernization. The clearest examples of this are to be found in Islamic countries, but there are traces in other cultures.

Fundamentalism exists in most religions, and the one thing they

Five

all have in common is control of women – especially women's sexuality – and the use of violence to impose this control. Violence is not only physical, but also psychological and even spiritual.

Political power is reinforced when it can be linked to religious beliefs, and religious groups use political connections to protect their interests. The symbiotic relationship between religion and politics can be lethal to women, as we have seen in many countries.

SAPs and women's movements

The IMF/World Bank-inspired programmes of structural adjustment adopted by many governments, starting with those in Latin America, from the 1980s onward, were particularly inimical to women. Although there were variations within the policy framework, structural adjustment policies did in fact constitute a specific policy package grounded in the ideology of neo-liberalism. Underlying this policy framework was an ideology of the role of the state (its relationship to its citizens) and a gender ideology (the social relations between men and women, and specifically, women's traditional role in domestic work and the care of people – social reproduction).

By the mid-1980s, these policies were also being introduced throughout the Caribbean and Africa. While South-East Asia's continued economic prosperity during the 1980s protected these countries, the collapse of major currencies in the region by the

---

Personal reflection

When I first analysed the impact of these policies on Jamaican women, using data from UNICEF within a conceptual framework formulated by DAWN, I described them as gender-blind. On further reflection, however, it became clear to me that these policies were actually grounded in a gender ideology that was deeply exploitative of women's time, labour and sexuality: women are conditioned to take care of people, and, knowing this, the state can cut social services.

mid-1990s led to the introduction of IMF-inspired policies of adjustment, despite mounting evidence of their disastrous consequences on the poor and other marginalized groups.

The Latin American feminist movements were the first to confront the socio-economic changes resulting from the introduction of policies of structural adjustment. Again, UNICEF was to take the lead by sponsoring the publication of a book written by Latin American feminist scholars, *The Invisible Adjustment* (UNICEF/LA, 1986), that highlighted how debt repayment was to be achieved by the 'super-exploitation' of women through their unwaged work in the household and low-paid jobs in the export-oriented industries.

Macro-economic policies which privilege economic production over social reproduction by cutting social services jeopardize women in three ways: first, by reducing employment, because it is women who predominate in the social sector; second, by reducing their access to services that are essential if they are to manage their dual roles in production and reproduction; and third, by increasing the demand on their time, as they are expected to fill the gaps created by the cuts.

Similarly, on the production side of the equation, the export-oriented production models focus in many instances on the creation of export-processing zones dependent on large supplies of cheap and compliant female labour, an ideal reserve labour force. The emphasis on export-oriented agriculture, meanwhile, jeopardized the production of food, the chief area of women's involvement in the field of agriculture and the chief source of nutrition for their families.

But the negative impact of these policies on women also highlighted how policies that hurt women spill over to the whole society. The centrality of women's role in reproduction, and the link between social reproduction and production, mean that policies that harm women undermine the economy and society in fundamental ways, affecting the health and nutrition of families, levels of productivity as well as the level of wages. Research in many countries shows how the exclusion of labour unions and the payment of exploitative wages to women in the export-processing zones serve to undermine both the unions and the wage levels for men. Many countries also reported increases in violence, including domestic violence, as displaced, disadvantaged and disenfranchised men took out their frustrations on women and children.

In fact, as many feminists were to point out, by privileging economic production over social development and reproduction, the policies undermined the very foundations of economic activity. Economic production is, after all, determined not only by natural resources, capital, technology and markets, but by the physical, intellectual and psychological capacities of the labour force, all determined in the sphere of social reproduction, a domain in which women's role is central.

The impact of the IMF-inspired neo-liberal macro-economic policy framework of structural adjustment on women's lives also drew attention to the workings of the IFIs, whose relation to US government policy (specifically the US Treasury) produced the Washington Consensus that was to become the dominant policy framework from this decade into the 21st century. Before the 1980s, there is little evidence that women's movements paid much attention to these institutions and the ways in which macro-economic frameworks and global trends impacted on women's lives.

These linkages, spread through the mechanisms of the IFIs, also enabled women to understand how the legacies of colonialism continued to operate in a post-colonial world, in a pattern of neo-colonial relationships that were to be more insidious than those of colonialism. In short, by providing a new conceptual framework and a more holistic analysis of the position and situation of women, the 1980s gave women's movements everywhere new ways of looking at the world, and a new understanding of how power relations between the countries of the North and South affected the policy frameworks adopted by their governments. This new understanding provided women's movements, particularly those of the economic South, with a deeper and wider analytical framework, and contributed to a shift from a narrow definition of 'women's issues' to formulations of 'women's perspectives' on the widest range of issues.

In Latin America, the introduction of these policies from

the mid-1980s, at a time when military dictatorships were being replaced by democratic institutions, facilitated the participation of women from the region in UN global conferences, and Latin American women made a special contribution to the understanding of the gender dimensions of these policies.

It was no surprise, therefore, that the critique of structural adjustment policies became a major focus for women's research, analysis, advocacy and organizing throughout the second half of the 1980s and into the 1990s. Indeed, women played a leadership role in research and advocacy around issues of structural adjustment. Using gender analysis and feminist perspectives in their research and analysis of these policies, women researchers and activists were to offer important insights into the conceptual foundations and negative consequences of these policies for the whole society.

Although, during the decade of the 1980s, these policies were being adopted mostly in Latin America and the Caribbean, research into the impact of the policies in that region was incorporated into the analyses of women throughout the world, and drew attention to the link between macro-economic policy and the daily lives of women everywhere. From 1987 onwards, the number of publications by feminist scholars and activists on the impact of SAPs on women was phenomenal. These policies launched a new field of enquiry. But the analytical framework and insights were first brought to the attention of the international women's movement by the DAWN group in their platform document prepared for Forum '85.

Third World women's analysis of SAPs The adoption of this document by women around the world was undoubtedly related to the process by which it was produced. Starting with a draft document prepared by Gita Sen, who had been a participant, with assistance from an associate, Caren Grown, the final platform document incorporated many of the comments offered by feminist researchers who had been working on these issues for years. But its impact was clearly related to the way in which the data were analysed. By introducing an analysis that related the daily

Personal reflection

In August 1984, on the eve of the Third UN Conference on Women scheduled to take place in Nairobi, Kenya, I was invited by the Indian economist, Devaki Jain, to a small meeting of women from different regions. The meeting was held in Bangalore. Its purpose was to prepare a platform document for the NGO forum that would parallel the conference. There were no prepared papers. Participants were simply invited to reflect on their experience of the Decade. As the women shared their stories, the word 'crisis' emerged as a theme. However, there were clear regional differences in the experience of crisis.

For the women from the Pacific, the crisis was related to the testing of nuclear weapons in the Pacific. Asian women spoke of the rise in fundamentalism that was threatening women's rights. African women focused on the crisis in food security. Latin American women were concerned about the impact on women of the policies of structural adjustment that were being introduced by their governments as conditions for accessing loans from the IMF. As we analysed these crises we came to see them as linked, and related to the dominant model of development, the growth model.

The document, *Development, Crises and Alternative Visions: Third World Women's Perspectives* (Sen and Grawn, 1976), explored the links between the systemic crises of debt, deteriorating services, environmental degradation, militarism, religious fundamentalism and political conservatism. The document formed the basis of a series of panels at the NGO Forum and was met with an overwhelming response. It was clearly an idea whose time had come.

experiences of women to colonial relations between countries and the macro-economic policy framework, and by revealing the systemic links between economic (colonialism and capitalism), political (patriarchy), social (gender relations) and cultural (religious fundamentalism) factors, DAWN gave women a new way of viewing global processes and development issues. This analysis was to change the terms of the debate on Women in Development (WID) and prepare women for analysing all issues from the perspective of women.

The document broke new ground. Up to this time women's issues had tended to be discussed in largely ahistorical and sectoral terms. For the first time at these events, women were exposed to a feminist analysis of the macro-economic policies of structural adjustment and their place in colonial and neo-colonial relations. This analysis, and the conceptual framework used by DAWN, were to change the movement's understanding of the link between colonial relations of dependence, macro-economic policy frameworks, and women's experience of crises in different aspects of their lives, in different parts of the world. The shift to a more holistic and political analysis of the issues, and DAWN's call for women's empowerment through their organizations as the basis for the kind of social change that would place people at the centre of the agenda, strengthened women's advocacy and

---

The characteristics of DAWN's analysis

- focus on the daily experiences of poor women living in the economic South;
- acknowledgement of regional diversity;
- linking of economic, social, cultural and political factors;
- attempt to link experience at the micro level of women's daily lives to an understanding of the macro-economic policy framework and global trends;
- understanding of the political nature of development;
- use of a feminist framework: rejecting dichotomies of personal and political, private and public domains; validating women's work, experience and knowledge; and working in solidarity with women.

contributed a framework that was to serve women well in their advocacy on the global issues that formed the agenda for the UN conferences of the 1990s.

Women's responses to 'the crisis' Because the debt crisis and policies of structural adjustment were experienced most sharply in Latin America in the 1980s, it is here that we can see most clearly the ways in which 'the crisis' served to mobilize women at community and national levels. From the establishment of soup kitchens to assist poor families, and the sharing of scarce resources, to the establishment of a variety of small business ventures within the informal sectors, and to the protests against rising food prices and cuts in social services, women responded with creative survival strategies as well as with political mobilization. Thus the 1980s provided Latin American and Caribbean women a unique opportunity for popular education and mobilization around the political economy of capitalism.

During the 1980s, and particularly after 1985, women became increasingly aware of the links between the economic, political, social and cultural consequences of the policy framework, and they brought this understanding to bear as they organized to participate in the global conferences of the 1990s.

Conclusion

Feminist analyses of the impact of the IMF-inspired structural adjustment policies that provided the policy framework during this decade, as well as women's responses to the socio-economic and political crises provoked by their introduction, led to new insights into the ways in which assumptions about gender roles were embedded in public policies. These insights gave women a better understanding of the ways in which their economies worked, and the role of international institutions in shaping national policies.

By introducing an analysis drawn from the experience of women who were the most marginalized, this leadership generated new perspectives and facilitated a shift from the original goal of 'integrating women in development' to 'empowering women for social change', from a focus on narrowly defined 'women's issues' to 'women's perspectives' on a range of issues of concern to everyone.

This understanding opened the way to the new forms of organizing and analysis that were to place women in a position to bring new perspectives to the global debates of the 1990s. Indeed, the analytical framework and methodology used in the formulation of critiques of these policies were critical to the evolution of a global women's movement.

Notes

1 A good example of this policy 'choice' was the adoption of this policy framework by a newly elected government in the small Caribbean island state of St Vincent in 1984. At that time St Vincent had no international debt of any significance. While it had a small deficit on current account, this was already being reduced when the new government took office. What encouraged the new government to introduce these policies was the influence of the IFIs on the regional development bank, which had announced that 'structural adjustment was the key to Caribbean economic transformation'. Thereafter, the government of St Vincent won continuous applause from the IFIs for having adopted the framework without any pressure on their part. This behaviour was considered an example of 'good governance', despite the fact that it ultimately led to the destruction of the economy, and to great indebtedness as foreign investors reneged on their obligations to repay loans underwritten by the government.

2 See Chapter 2 for how the shift in policy frameworks was reflected in shifts in the relative importance of international institutions.

3 Although in many cases these policies also failed to produce the economic results used to justify them: many countries saw their economies stagnate and collapse under policies aimed at cutting government budgets and increasing unemployment in the name of curbing inflation – whether or not this existed.

6 | It's about justice: feminist leadership making a difference on the world stage

Background to the global conferences of the 1990s

If the Decade for Women generated the activities and commitment that nurtured local women's movements and gave birth to an international women's movement, and the 1980s enabled women to understand the links between their reality and the larger political, economic, social and cultural structures that framed that experience, the decade of the 1990s provided the stage on which this international movement announced itself as a global political constituency, a global women's movement. Women from around the world who had been actively engaged in the UN women's conferences of the Decade for Women seized the opportunity to participate in the ensuing debates and attempt to redefine and redesign agendas to meet their visions of a better world.

With the interesting exception of the Children's Summit in 1990, in which the international women's movement was noticeably, and significantly, absent, women's movements from around the world mobilized for engagement in the global conferences on

---

Personal reflection

The city of Rio de Janeiro holds special significance for me. It was where the DAWN network was formally launched in 1986, following the response to our panels at the 1985 conference in Nairobi. In 1990 the DAWN steering committee met again in Rio, to review our operations and to select a new General Coordinator. Accepting the responsibility of General Coordinator gave me a unique vantage point from which to witness the emergence of women as a political constituency on the stage of the global conferences of the 1990s.

Environment (Rio 1992), Human Rights (Vienna 1993), Population (Cairo 1994), Poverty (Copenhagen 1995), Habitat (Istanbul 1996) and Food (Rome 1997).

This chapter will be organized around the themes of economic justice, gender justice and political justice as they played out in the global conferences of the 1990s and beyond. The questions to be addressed in this chapter are:

- What are the positions of women's movements on the key issues of economic, social/gender and political justice, and how were these articulated by a global women's movement during the global conferences of the 1990s and beyond?
- How did these positions differ from those of their governments and male-dominated NGOs?
- How did the global women's movement affect the debate at these conferences?

I will argue that, building on the analysis and experience of organizing across national, disciplinary and thematic boundaries throughout the Decade for Women, the leadership of feminist activists succeeded in changing the terms and outcomes of the global debates of the 1990s, in ways that clarified linkages between social, cultural, economic and political factors and pointed the way to more credible solutions to problems of environmental degradation, sustainable livelihoods, poverty, human rights and population.

The themes and debates Although the categories of economic, social/gender and political justice will be used, the links between these are always acknowledged. Indeed, the most cursory review of the debates would show both how the categories are inextricably linked and how the differences in positions taken by different networks invariably related to the failure to adopt a holistic analysis of the different issues. The categories cover the following:

- *economic justice* includes environment, sustainable development, livelihoods and trade;

81

- *gender justice* covers women's human rights, including sexual and reproductive rights and violence against women;
- *political justice* includes democracy, power relations between women and men, women and the state, and the concepts of 'good governance' and an 'enabling environment'.

Economic justice: the UN Conference on Environment and Development (UNCED)

Setting the stage: the issues The UN Conference on Environment and Development (UNCED) marked the opening up of the UN to participation, on a new scale, by representatives of civil society. These included representatives of women's organizations, and individual women who had been working together throughout the Decade for Women. Together with women from other NGOs, particularly from the environmental organizations, they formed a constituency that was different from the more traditional women's organizations that had long enjoyed consultative status at the UN.

Personal reflection

Towards the end of 1990 I was invited by Bella Abzug to be part of an international policy advisory committee that she was convening to prepare for the upcoming UN Conference on Environment and Development (UNCED). Bella, an experienced congresswoman and leader in the women's movement in her country, had achieved notoriety when she had been dismissed from a Presidential Task Force on women for straying from the strict terms of her mandate on women's issues to raise questions about the President's budget. This was not considered a 'women's issue'.

The World Women's Congress for a Healthy Planet attracted an international audience of over 1,500 women. It was organized as a tribunal, each session having a panel of international speakers (women considered experts on their topic) who were interrogated by a panel of international

---

judges (each prominent in the judiciary of her country). The participants were the 'jury', prohibited from asking questions but charged with reaching conclusions on the issues presented and drafting the recommendations that were to form a 'Women's Agenda 21'.

My topic, on the first panel, carried the innocuous title, 'The Real World of Women', a clear indication of my lack of specific expertise when placed beside well-known activists such as Vandana Shiva (Indian physicist), Rosalie Bertell (Canadian biologist) and Marilyn Waring (New Zealand economist).[1] I was to be the last speaker, preceded by a banker from Sierra Leone who spoke on the Uruguay Round of trade negotiations.[2] The gist of this presentation was that, if these negotiations succeeded, all environmental problems would be solved by the magic of a liberalized market that would 'get prices right' and thereby reduce or prevent environmental degradation.

The audience expressed their disbelief of this position with shocked gasps and whispers. They could see the flaws in the speaker's argument, but could not express them because of the way in which the session was structured. Unfortunately the judges could not help: they did not know the right questions. It was left to me to give voice to the concerns of the audience. Before the conference I had been struck by the fact that the two sets of global negotiations that were taking place at the time, the Uruguay Round and those focused on the Earth Summit, were being conducted along separate tracks. I could see the connections, specifically that trade liberalization would make it very difficult for governments to protect their environments. I said this and the audience rose to its feet. I knew then that an international women's movement had come of age. The audience had recognized instantly the contradictions inherent in policies that promoted trade liberalization and those that sought to protect the environment.[3]

While the mainstream approach to environmental issues tended to be largely scientific, technical and abstract – macro issues such as global warming and environmental pollution – women's approaches tended to be grounded in their own experience. In the USA the focus was apt to be on the impact of pollution on women's health while, in developing countries, the focus tended to be on water, health and livelihoods (including access to land). Using women's daily experience as the starting point for an analysis of environmental degradation produced a wide array of issues that were ultimately linked to the way in which the economy was organized.

In developing countries, access to land, forests and rivers was crucial for survival. And yet poor people did not destroy their environments. They did not have the technology to wreak the damage that could result from the use of large-scale technology and equipment. As the saying went: women cannot destroy the forest; they only pick up the twigs left in the wake of the bulldozers. Moreover, one could ask: Why would anyone choose to live and farm on marginal lands? An examination of the conditions under which poor people were forced to live highlighted, as nothing else could, the link between the reality of poor women's lives and capitalist expansion and exploitation under colonialism and neo-colonialism, where the best land was appropriated for those connected to the centres of power and privilege, leaving the majority of people to fend for themselves on marginal lands.

India's experience was a source of information and inspiration for many women from the industrialized countries coming to an understanding of environmental issues for the first time. Vandana Shiva's critique in *Staying Alive* was to become a basic reference and rallying point for the environmental movement. Her description of the destruction of indigenous seeds by the introduction of genetically modified varieties introduced many women to the threats faced by poor farmers who could not afford to purchase commercial seeds after their indigenous varieties were destroyed by 'killer' technologies. Activism to prevent the destruction of villages to build the Narmada dam in India helped women understand the tension between those who would benefit from tech-

84

nological advances and those who would lose; while the Chipko movement of women, who hugged trees to protect them from the bulldozers intent on clearing land for 'development', provided insight into the complexities of the trade-offs between economic growth and social development. Finally, women from the Pacific drew attention to the massive destruction of environments, health and livelihoods caused by the testing of nuclear weapons in their region, and how the ability of the governments of the USA and France in particular to use this region for these tests arose from the colonial and neo-colonial relations that existed between these world powers and many of the islands in the region. In these and other instances, a focus on the experience of poor women in the economic South exposed the relationship between environmental issues and prevailing political and economic models.

DAWN's regional consultations Seeking regional perspectives on the environmental crisis, DAWN found that many of the issues raised during reflections on the development model at their first meeting in 1984 were repeated in regional consultations between 1990–91: women from the Pacific again highlighted the threat to their lives and livelihood of nuclear testing in their region, while African women related issues of food security to desertification. In Asia and Latin America, deforestation was the major concern of poor women, while for the Caribbean the overuse of pesticides in banana cultivation was seen as a health hazard to women and their infant children. In all parts of the South, rapid urbanization related to economic growth posed special problems for women and their families.

At a regional consultation in the Caribbean, a participant summed up the links between the personal and the political thus, 'Our first environment is our bodies, ourselves, and the land that sustains us.' Discussion of the environmental concerns of poor women focuses on health and livelihoods and the political economy that determines their access to both. An analysis of the factors affecting health and livelihoods at the micro level of women's daily lives points to links between the debt crisis and macro-economic policies of structural adjustment that cut services and subsidies to the poor, as well as to those between the lucrative trade in arms, the colonial relations that make it impossible for small island states to protect their natural environments, and the testing of nuclear weapons that destroy the lives of people and their ecosystems.

In every instance, women argued that it was impossible to understand the problem of environmental degradation without understanding economic, political, social and cultural factors. Women applying this holistic analysis and linking women's daily experience to the macro-economic policy framework and global trends came up with a very different analysis of the problem and what needed to be done from that of their governments and other environmental NGOs.

The conference and Forum At the NGO Forum in Rio, women's groups converged on the 'Women's Tent' organized by the Women, Environment and Development Organization (WEDO), launched by Bella Abzug following the meeting in Miami. In addition to the rich programme of panels, workshops and exhibitions presented there, the Tent became the focal point for women's networking and organizing, and for the formulation of positions that were then negotiated with mainstream NGOs as well as with government delegations at the conference.

DIFFERENCES While governments of the South focused on extracting more money from the North for development that would 'protect the environment for future generations' ('sustainable development'), women from the South argued for a different, more sustainable, approach to development, one that would sustain the livelihoods of the poor and protect health. While governments of the North argued for the development and use of cleaner technologies in economic production, and for pricing mechanisms that could be used to ration the use of scarce resources, women from North and South, along with some NGOs, drew attention to the wasteful and harmful consumption patterns of the rich that used a disproportionate amount of resources. They called on the privileged to exercise restraint, and they called for distributive justice that would improve the consumption of the poor.

There were differences between NGOs as well. While mainstream NGO discussions focused on the formulation of alternative treaties to be negotiated with governments, women's organizations and networks worked on a broader array of initiatives. The Women's Agenda 21 was one such initiative, and it is interesting to see the ways in which this document was to differ from the main Agenda 21.[4] Another was the launching of 'environmental audits' to be conducted by grassroots women. It was recognized that women everywhere were making important contributions to the adoption of better conservation practices, and sharing information through their networks.

Powerful environmental groups from the North tended to view poor people as a 'problem' for the environment. Malthusian nightmares of overpopulation were conjured up to make the link between the 'carrying capacity' of the earth and population pressures. On the other hand, organizations of indigenous peoples, and NGOs representing them, saw the problem as one of capitalist exploitation and appropriation of ancestral lands and rights. A focus on the environmental practices of poor women showed clearly that, far from exploiting their environment, they were more likely to protect it with practices that were conservative and sustainable. Indeed, poor women were blamed both for 'having too many children' (as if they made this 'choice' by themselves) and for 'destroying the forests' (as if they could produce as much damage to forests as bulldozers).

In its platform document for the Women's Tent at the NGO

The four myths about environmental degradation

- the poor are destroying the environment.
- Population growth is responsible for environmental degradation.
- Lack of knowledge is responsible for environmental degradation.
- Structural adjustment will set right the problems of poverty, employment and environment.

Forum in Rio, DAWN addressed these and other issues by exposing four myths. DAWN showed clearly the links between government policies and environmental degradation, and why blaming women for environmental crisis because of high fertility rates and their need to draw on environmental resources would not solve the problem.

After UNCED, the global women's movement's on-going work on environmental issues was linked to work on sustainable development and specifically to work on poverty eradication – 'sustaining the livelihoods of the poor' – and the promotion of a framework of social and economic rights.

World Summit for Social Development (WSSD) The World Summit for Social Development (WSSD), held in Copenhagen in March 1995, provided the global women's movement with another opportunity to address the economic framework that denies fundamental social and economic rights to the majority of the world's people. By that time women had a clear sense of the contradictions inherent in an economic model geared to the maximization of profits while promising employment and poverty reduction. In addition, following the International Conference on Human Rights in 1993 and the International Conference on Population and Development (ICPD), which had taken place a year earlier, a framework that emphasized the universality and indivisibility of rights, including women's sexual and reproductive rights, had become the overarching model for addressing poverty.

At WSSD, women's advocacy focused on a critique of structural adjustment, and on showing why the continued promotion of such a policy framework could not provide an 'enabling environment' at national or international levels, either for poverty reduction, employment creation and the achievement of social security (the themes of WSSD), or for the implementation of the commitments to women's health, rights and empowerment that were made at ICPD.[5] While strong alliances were formed with the male-led NGOs that were contesting the economic policy framework, these NGOs continued to ignore the broader agenda that included women's human rights.[6]

Alternative economic frameworks – DAWN's platform for the Fifth World Women's Conference In their platform document for the Beijing conference, *Markers on the Way: The DAWN Debates on Alternative Development*, DAWN launched a critique of the market and defined a three-pronged strategy for South-based women's movements: reform the state, challenge the market and build the capacity of civil society to do both, from the perspectives of marginalized women.[7] Women's movements were beginning to recognize the capacity of the market-driven, globalized economic model to affect their lives more profoundly than ever before.

At the conference and Forum, women pushed for the adoption of a women's human rights framework that would underscore the universality and indivisibility of women's rights. This framework will be discussed later in the chapter.

Trade issues With the launching of the World Trade Organization (WTO), the central arena for global negotiations shifted from the UN and the IFIs to the WTO. This inter-governmental organization was destined to become the most powerful of the international institutions because of its ability to enforce its rulings by imposing sanctions on states; its operations were to have more profound impacts on women's lives than those of any other international agency.

The International Gender and Trade Network (IGTN) The recognition, going forward from the Beijing conference, that trade was an issue of critical importance for women was reflected in the launching of IGTN. IGTN's strategy links research and economic literacy in economics and trade to advocacy. The work of regional networks is coordinated through an international steering committee (IGTN) comprised of regional representatives along with coordinators for the programmes of research and literacy. At the heart of IGTN's advocacy is rejection of the premise that free trade can be beneficial to all countries and all sectors within countries. Building on the earlier analyses of structural adjustment, IGTN emphasizes the differential impact of trade policy and practice on women and men and calls for special attention

89

Personal reflection

Early in 1998 I was approached by Maria Riley of the Center of Concern, a Jesuit think tank in Washington DC, about co-sponsoring a strategic planning meeting on gender and trade as a first step towards organizing women for engagement in trade negotiations. She described how she had become increasingly concerned about the fact that the international women's movement was absent from these negotiations, which were to have such an impact on our lives.

As a result, DAWN Caribbean co-sponsored the International Women's Strategic Planning Workshop on Gender and Trade, which led to the launching of the International Gender and Trade Network (IGTN). It was held in Grenada following the ground-breaking Second Ministerial Meeting of the WTO in Seattle.

to be paid to the impact of trade on social reproduction, i.e. on people's access to food and to the services 'essential to social reproduction'.

While IGTN builds alliances with other NGOs that have a critical approach to the WTO, the network's primary purpose in relation to these groups is to sensitize them to issues of concern to women within these processes. This is no easy task, given the persistent and pervasive sexism that exists within NGOs as well as within governments, even among women in these spaces.

DIFFERENCES As in other issues, there are at least two approaches to women and trade. One is to strengthen the participation of women in trade, to work towards enhancing the opportunities for women to benefit from trade liberalization. The other is to consider the ways in which trade liberalization affects women's lives, especially those of poor, marginalized women and their families, inevitably left behind in the wake of the tidal wave of economic globalization.

The first approach is reflected in UNIFEM's work in this area.

As early as 1997 UNIFEM had launched a series of regional seminars and workshops on women and trade. These seminars focused on women's participation in trade and on the challenges and opportunities presented by the new trade agreements for women. The second, more critical, approach recognized that the new trade agenda would have to be considered in relation to socio-economic development and the role of the state, and aimed at showing how trade liberalization would affect marginalized populations in the North and South. Using an analytical framework drawn from feminist political economy, and drawing on what was known of the impact of neo-liberalism on countries of the South, this approach underlined the ways in which the new trade agreements, grounded as they are in the neo-liberal paradigm, are inconsistent with goals of equity and sustainability.

In the debates around trade, the differences between women's networks critical of the neo-liberalism framework and those that seek to mainstream women into this framework parallel earlier debates between those who advocated integrating women in development, and those who adopted a more critical approach. However, both approaches are consistent within a global women's movement that simultaneously seeks reform and revolutionary change, integration within the mainstream and an option to remain outside and work for more fundamental change.

Gender justice

International Conference on Human Rights, Vienna 1993: preparatory process – the campaign The UN Conference on Human Rights provided a special opportunity for an international women's movement to insert its concerns into the UN framework. Among the early preparations for the conference was a campaign to emphasize that women's rights are human rights. Under the leadership of feminist activist Charlotte Bunch of the Center for Women's Global Leadership (CWGL) at Rutgers University, the campaign was launched with a worldwide petition, circulated in late 1991, demanding that the conference take women into account with regard to human rights issues in general, and that it address violence against women in particular. According to the organizers, 250,000 people from 120 countries signed the petition. The campaign worked in two ways: it alerted women all over the world to human rights issues, and mobilized them to influence the Vienna conference. It also helped disseminate information about the Vienna conference.

A related activity was a strategic planning institute, convened by CWGL. It brought together twenty-five women from around the world who were engaged in campaigns in their own countries to get the UN to recognize women's rights as human rights. Participants drafted strategies and actions in relation to the conference, and agreed to organize a Global Tribunal on Violations of Women's Human Rights with a view to influencing the conference. This was followed by a series of international leadership institutes that provided opportunities for women human rights activists from different countries to design guidelines for the on-going campaigns to raise women's awareness of their human rights by relating their own experience of abuse to the rights framework. Local tribunals made it possible for the widest diversity of women to participate in refining a women's human rights framework, and served to enrich global advocacy. The campaign set a new standard for linking work at local and global levels.

Among the many meetings held in preparation for this conference was one convened by the Ottawa-based North–South Institute. Entitled 'Linking Hands for Changing Law: Women's Rights as Human Rights Around the World', the meeting brought together more than a hundred women's human rights activists and specialists to 'look at the inadequacy of the present human rights model to guarantee women's human rights' (Joanna Kerr, North–South Institute, 1992).

This meeting was to lead to a number of other initiatives to place women's rights on the agenda of the conference. One of these was the formation of an organization of Latin American and Caribbean women, 'La Nuestra' (That Which is Ours), which met to draft a proposal on women's human rights to take to the UN regional preparatory meeting held in Costa Rica in January 1993. At this meeting the feminist radio station, FIRE, broadcast live, 'bringing to the international audience the fact that women were determined to make the UN recognize our needs and interests in their agenda for human rights'.[8]

The conference and tribunal The Global Tribune on Violations of Women's Human Rights was convened by a broad coalition of women's groups, and coordinated by CWGL and the International Women's Tribune Centre. It was the result of the efforts of thousands of women's organizations and networks around the world, joining together to demand an end to the impunity surrounding women's human rights abuses. The presence of women telling their own stories of experiences from domestic violence to female genital mutilation and war crimes strengthened women's advocacy in Vienna and guaranteed that women's concerns would be taken into account at the conference. It placed violence against women on the agenda of a human rights conference for the first time.[9]

By removing the veil from violence that takes place in the household, the concept of women's human rights advances understanding of human rights by foreclosing the distinction between the 'private' sphere of the household, and the 'public' sphere where only state-perpetrated violence is considered. The UN and governments had failed to recognize the abuses of women's bodies because they were considered private, family, cultural or religious matters.

A special chapter on women's human rights was included in the programme of action adopted by the conference, and the UN General Assembly adopted the Declaration on the Elimination of Violence Against Women later in the same year. The appointment by the UN Commission on Human Rights of a special rapporteur to investigate violence against women and report to the Commission with proposals for addressing the issue, provided a framework for monitoring progress on the Declaration.

An outcome of the experience leading up to the conference and at the Forum and conference itself was the strengthening of work on women's human rights networks in all regions. The assertion that 'women's rights are human rights' and the expansion of the rights framework to incorporate explicitly sexual and reproductive rights, along with economic and social rights, provided a solid base for further advocacy by the emerging global women's movement.

One of the most important outcomes of the work of the global women's movement is the placing of the issue of violence against women on the agenda as a violation of women's human rights. The Declaration on the Elimination of Violence Against Women reflects this, while the annual 'Sixteen Days of Activism Against Gender Violence Campaign' that takes place in the run-up to the November 25 Day Against Violence Against Women establishes a context in which women can express their 'zero tolerance' for violence.

It is the context in which, in recent years, revelations by a Women's International War Crimes Tribunal on Japan's military sexual slavery and the widespread use of rape and forced impregnation of Muslim women in the former Yugoslavia have forced powerful governments to pay attention to these violations of women's human rights and take action to protect women from these abuses in the future. The classification of rape as a war crime is a major advance, and a necessary first step towards the enforcement of measures designed to protect women in situations of armed conflict. The gender-specific abuse of women who live in refugee camps or in prisons is another issue receiving attention.

Another important advance is the increasing understanding of violence against women and children as part of a continuum that has its roots in sexism. This understanding has implications for peace studies and for projects aimed at the promotion of human security.

DIFFERENCES Although violence against women is an issue that unites women around the world, not all feminist activists agree that the human rights route and reliance on legal systems can deliver justice to women who have experienced extreme forms of gender-based abuse. The Courts of Women organized by Corinne Kumar and her associates represent an alternative approach to bringing relief to women who have been victims of abuse and structural violence.[10] These courts have underscored the wide range of abuses of women's human rights – from the abuse of 'comfort' women by the Japanese to the deprivations experienced by women and children under Israeli occupation in the Palestinian territories and because of the US embargo of Cuba, from the rape of women in the former Yugoslavia to racism and colonization. What the abused women seek is not an easy judgment passed down by a court of law but rather an acknowledgement of their crimes by the perpetrators, and an apology for the immeasurable harm caused to the women, their families and communities.

Women's organizing around the 1993 International Conference on Human Rights set the stage for the broadening of the rights framework that was to prove critical to bringing together traditional women's rights advocates and activists from developing countries who focused on socio-economic issues.

Sexual and reproductive rights The first alerts to the looming struggle over women's sexual and reproductive health and rights were heard at UNCED. In the process around UNCED women's movements were already beginning to experience the repercussions of the Malthusian equation of population pressure and environmental degradation. When this was linked to the critiques of demographically driven population policies and abusive family planning practices that were gathering steam, and the Vatican's positioning to align itself with these, women's rights advocates knew that they faced a major and complex challenge.

Critiques of demographically driven population policies One of the sharpest divisions within women's movements, and one of the most difficult for a global women's movement to resolve, has been, and continues to be, the division between feminists who are uncompromising in their rejection of new reproductive technologies and those who, while recognizing the abuses to which women, especially poor women from the South, have been subjected from racist and coercive demographically driven population policies and programmes, nevertheless argue that reproductive health programmes must be safe, affordable and accessible for all women.

Personal reflection

On my flight from the Rio at the end of UNCED, I finally had a chance to read the final Forum newspapers. Two articles highlighted the problems that were going to confront women at the upcoming International Conference on Population and Development (ICPD). While the article written by the head of the UN Fund for Population Activities (UNFPA) bought into the argument that population pressures were a major source of damage to the environment, the Vatican's representative argued cleverly – as did progressive NGOs, including the women's movement – that what was needed was an alternative development paradigm, one guided by equity and ethical values. If I did not know the Vatican's position on women I might have aligned myself with their statement.

It was clear that the Vatican had positioned itself as champion of the South! What the Vatican said was impeccable. It was the Vatican's relationship with feminist organizations[11] that alerted me to the potential problems that we might face as we moved into the next stages of global negotiations around the issue of population. For, by aligning with women advocates who refused to blame women's fertility for environmental degradation, and those who were advocating strongly against harmful reproductive technologies, the Vatican was also positioning itself to argue against women's reproductive rights in the ICPD process.

The DAWN network was one of the latter. Reproductive rights and population had been identified as a theme at the 1990 meeting, and Brazilian feminist health activist Sonia Correa had been selected as research coordinator. DAWN's holistic analysis showed that women's health could not be considered in isolation from the economic, political, social and cultural conditions of their lives. DAWN's earlier work for the 1985 Forum had noted how macro-economic policies of structural adjustment had led to cuts in health services and showed how the political conservatism associated with the promotion of these neo-liberal policies also allied with forces of the religious right to reverse gains made in women's reproductive health and rights. DAWN's platform for ICPD, *Population and Reproductive Rights: Perspectives from the South*,[12] built on this earlier work.

International Conference on Population and Development, Cairo 1994 preparatory process The potential of an alliance between religious fundamentalists and those in the women's movement who were justifiably critical of demographically driven population policies alerted some of us to the dangers to women's lives in the processes leading up to ICPD. The position of the family planning establishment, with its emphasis on contraceptive targets, added complexity to the problems facing those in the global women's movement who sensed the dangers. To prepare for what was expected to be a contentious and complex set of negotiations around these issues, a network, 'Women's Voices for Cairo', was formed, to build a consensus for a population policy that would acknowledge and affirm women's right to control their fertility, and meet their needs for safe, affordable and accessible contraceptives.

Between 1991 and 1994 DAWN and others in the international women's health movement worked to bridge the ideological gap between these different groups of women. It was not an easy struggle, and demanded the utmost of skills in research, analysis, advocacy and, most of all, leadership. At the beginning of 1994 DAWN worked with the US-based International Women's Health Coalition (IWHC) to organize an international strategy meeting (in Rio) that prepared women to participate in the difficult process of producing a document for ICPD that would reflect women's concerns. Participants from this meeting then worked within the processes leading up to the conference to change the draft document accordingly, and to engage in the even more difficult task of building political will among governments. This was especially difficult for women from developing countries, since some of the most conservative governments were members of G-77. In addition to all this, as we had feared, the Vatican built a coalition with Islamic fundamentalists to discredit and undermine the conference itself. In the end it was only by persuading supportive G-77 members to abandon the consensus rule, thus freeing them to negotiate with some strength, that a Programme of Action that reflected women's concerns was finally adopted.[13]

The new framework The new framework of women's Health, Empowerment, Rights and Accountability reflected in the Programme of Action of the ICPD, is a tribute to the feminists who forged these alliances against the forces of religious fundamentalism and political conservatism. Despite the efforts of the Vatican to characterize this conference as one focused on 'abortion and same-sex marriage', the framework negotiated at ICPD was much wider than the narrow focus on family planning and contraception at earlier conferences on this theme.

The struggle to protect the framework However, there was a price to pay for the success of feminist organizing in Cairo. The success of the progressive women's movement in securing the new framework[14] provoked an on-going campaign, led by the Vatican and its allies, to reverse the cumulative gains made by women. This became clear in the conferences held the following year: the World Summit on Social Development (WSSD) held in Copenhagen, and the Fourth World Conference on Women held in Beijing; and continued into the five-year reviews of ICPD and the Beijing conference.[15] In a paper commissioned by UNIFEM at the start of the five-year reviews, DAWN summed up the situation as follows:

> In the years 1998–99 the global women's movement had the opportunity to witness the complexity of the task it had set itself. Facing the challenges of a skilful and well-financed fundamentalist backlash combined with the hardening of North–South divisions on issues of economic justice, Third World women were confronted with many of their governments' willingness to trade gender justice for economic justice – a new manifestation of the dichotomising of the issues of production and reproduction.[16]

In the second half of the 1990s, as Third World countries came under increasing pressure from the spread of neo-liberalism through the IFIs and, increasingly, the WTO, the need for G-77 solidarity became more imperative. In this context the Vatican emerged as the champion of those marginalized by this policy framework. In addition, Roman Catholic leadership in the successful Jubilee campaign for Third World debt forgiveness gave the Vatican even greater clout among members of the G-77, and in the 1999 and 2000 five-year reviews of the conferences of the mid-1990s the women's movement was confronted with the reality that many of the G-77 countries that had supported them in 1994 and 1995 were no longer willing to do so.[17]

The spread of religious fundamentalism, which had often accompanied the socio-economic decline that followed in the wake of structural adjustment and neo-liberalism (economic fundamentalism), became more obvious in the latter half of the decade of the 1990s, and is a major factor in any consideration of political justice for women from this time, and for the foreseeable future.

Political justice

The context for women's relationship with the state: economic and religious fundamentalism While none of the global conferences of the 1990s addressed politics and governance directly, these were central to every issue discussed. In the context of the UN, every plan, platform or programme of action is addressed to governments, and contains a section specifically on the role of the state in the implementation of the plan. At UN conferences, women's movements engage their state as well as the international system of global governance. Relationships between women and the state are inevitably mediated by patriarchal norms at local as well as international levels, and women's engagements with the state and the multilateral system are shaped by gender politics at both these levels.

Throughout the decade of the 1990s, women's organizing took place in the context of two contradictory trends: on the one hand, as has been shown above, an increasingly confident global women's movement succeeded to a large extent in advancing

It's about justice

policy frameworks in the area of women's rights. At the same time, neo-liberalism and a rising tide of religious fundamentalism worked against these advances.

In Chapter 5, I tried to show how religious fundamentalism accompanied the decline in socio-economic conditions characteristic of neo-liberalism, and how this was exacerbated by the spread of Westernization inherent in globalization. Earlier in this chapter I referred to the fundamentalist backlash that followed the successful negotiation of sexual and reproductive rights in the conferences of the first half of the 1990s. With the triumph of the religious right in US elections in 2000, what had been a strong ally for the global women's movement in its struggle with fundamentalist forces in the ICPD process became a relentless opponent, reinforcing opposition to women's rights.

Religious fundamentalism undermines the very basis for women's organizing. As an important factor in most societies and as an aspect of socialization, religion reinforces the subordination of women within the patriarchal household, conditioning women and men to accept and internalize asymmetric gender relations, and robbing women of agency. This explains why many women act in accordance with societal norms that restrict their agency, thereby reproducing their own subordination. The distinction between male-defined and women-defined women is a useful one in understanding the political differences between those women who accept the status quo of male privilege and entitlement, and those who challenge it; and in explaining why women can act against their gender interests. This makes negotiations with state parties extremely difficult, in the global arena no less than at local levels.

A parallel between religious and economic fundamentalism can be seen when one considers the ways in which they are both grounded in the exploitation of women's time, labour and sexuality, robbing women of options and agency.[18] A discussion of political justice for women is therefore best understood in the context of these two fundamentalisms – socio-cultural and economic.

The 'marketization' of governance: good governance and the enabling environment The triumph of the market after the collapse of the Soviet Union, and the spread of neo-liberalism in the 1990s, led increasingly to a restructuring of political processes and the role of the state towards a political system that would serve the interests of international capital rather than the needs of those who had been excluded both economically and politically from the benefits of economic growth.[19] Increasingly the ideal of the 'people-friendly' state was replaced by the 'market-friendly' state. To the extent that poor women depend on the state for the guarantee of basic services, this shift has a devastating effect on these women, and those for whose care they are responsible.

This 'marketization'[20] of governance was accompanied, in the policy frameworks of the UN and the IFIs, by the concept of 'good' governance. Ostensibly it was a concept that focused on efficiency in management, the elimination of corruption, government transparency and accountability; however, no one could seriously claim that the private sector was any less corrupt, more transparent or more accountable than governments. It was clear the concept was a buzzword, used to distract attention from the real reasons for lack of progress on programmes and platforms of action: the lack of political will.

Another buzzword of the 1990s was the concept of the 'enabling economic environment', code for an uncritical acceptance of neo-liberalism as the framework to facilitate implementation of the recommendations adopted at the various global conferences.

Some feminists[21] attempted to draw attention to the fact that the political, social and economic environment created by neo-liberalism and globalization was anything but enabling for attempts to address problems of poverty, employment, social security, environment degradation or any of the other concerns that the conferences of the 1990s had addressed. For these feminists, an enabling environment would mean that:

- priority is given to the direction of resources to meeting the needs of the poorest and most vulnerable groups in society;

- imbalances of power are mediated by structures of governance to ensure all men and women have equal access;
- governments are responsive to issues emerging from dialogue with self-organized communities;
- women's experience and perspectives would be taken into account in the design and implementation of programmes of particular concern to them;
- at community and national levels mechanisms are in place to allow for continuous processes of negotiating consensus and mediating conflict, allowing for the creation and re-creation of sustainable livelihoods.

Assessment of the global conferences of the 1990s

Together the themes and discussions of the global conferences of the 1990s can be viewed as an indictment of an approach to socio-economic development that had patently failed to meet the goals of social justice and environmental protection. The analyses and critiques contributed by feminist-led women's movements to the discussions also highlighted the fact that these themes are inextricably linked; their separation prevents the kind of holistic analysis that might lead to more meaningful solutions. The links established in the Platform for Action of ICPD between women's health, rights and empowerment and the kind of enabling economic environment required to implement the recommendations of the platform is an example of what is possible when feminists have the opportunity to define the agenda. At the same time, even this formulation omitted the sharp critique of the economic and religious fundamentalisms that would inevitably block implementation of the recommendations.

This leads us to consider the limitations of inter-governmental debates staged within the framework of the UN. The search for consensus inevitably leads to a dilution of the arguments and to an acceptance of the 'smallest common denominator' in the ensuing recommendations. At the same time, a review of the outcomes of the conferences shows that it is easier to effect change when economic and political power is not directly challenged. The distinction made initially by Maxine Molyneux between practical and strategic gender issues is useful here: it is easier to effect changes that relate to practical gender issues, such as women's education and health (other than reproductive health, which is related to women's strategic gender interests), than it is to challenge the requirements of neo-liberal economic policy frameworks, local or global. The most frustrating aspect of UN debates is their refusal, or inability, to get consensus on a critique of the neo-liberal policy framework. Without this there are really no grounds for assuming that most recommendations can be implemented.

Similarly, in the area of human rights, it has been easier to argue for civil and political rights for women than to advance the agenda for social and economic rights, or for sexual and reproductive rights. The relentless attempts by the religious right in the USA and other fundamentalist forces to reverse gains negotiated by feminists during the conferences of the 1990s serve to remind us that the struggle for women's rights will be on-going, and of the need for constant vigilance. A global women's movement has a special role to play in monitoring these trends and serving as a focal point for mobilizations by local movements as they attempt to hold their governments accountable for the implementation of advances negotiated and adopted by the international community.

Where we were at the end of the 1990s: development and human rights paradigms In discussing the evolution of the global women's movement between the launching of the Decade for Women and the global conferences of the 1990s, some writers have described a shift from a 'development' paradigm, which 'dominated the Decade for Women', to a 'human rights' paradigm in the 1990s.[22] However, to do so is to ignore the ways in which the two are inextricably linked. While it is true that the discourse on women's condition and position seemed to focus on socio-economic issues during the Decade, issues of women's equality were always present in the discussion, and were indeed captured in the themes of the Decade – Equality, Development and Peace. At the same time, throughout the conferences of the 1990s issues of socio-economic development continued to be central concerns for marginalized women from both North and South – poverty and sustainable livelihoods, health, macro-economic policy and employment, food and housing. Indeed, from 1985 onwards, when DAWN developed its critiques of the growth-oriented model of development and the policy framework of structural adjustment, the analytical framework that formed the basis for approaches to the women's rights discourse was based on new understandings of the link between women's social and economic rights and our civic and political rights, as well as how cultural relativism affects the full range of women's human rights. This integration of the development paradigm with the rights paradigm can be seen as one of the achievements of the global women's movement.

Conclusion

During the 1990s the UN provided an unparalleled space for the nurturing and strengthening of a truly global women's movement. Women's participation in the global conferences of the 1990s demonstrated the potential of women as a political constituency determined to achieve a more inclusive social justice. Women's perspectives, analyses and advocacy demonstrated a different world view, which shed new light on ancient and persistent problems of poverty, marginality, human rights abuse and environmental degradation. At the same time the spread of neo-liberalism and fundamentalism threaten to erode the gains made by women's movements under the leadership of the emerging global women's movement.

The current crisis in governance includes a crisis in global governance in relation to economic as well as gender justice. In terms of economic justice, there is increasing concern among NGOs and civil society organizations at the growing 'coherence' between the policies of the IFIs, the WTO and even the UN as they push relentlessly for neo-liberalism. While this trend had been growing since the 1980s, it has become more entrenched in recent years. Most recently, at the 2003 World Summit on Sustainable Development (WSSD), the follow-up to UNCED, we witnessed the triumph of neo-liberalism in its most blatant form to date: the WTO-based trade regime has replaced the responsibility of states to provide a framework for the promotion of growth, the reduction of poverty and the protection of the environment; and public–private partnerships are now promoted to develop guidelines for, and monitor, implementation of the agenda. The WSSD also witnessed the virtual abandonment of Agenda 21 with its references to women's role in sustainable development, women's rights, and to sharing the costs of social reproduction.

The global women's movement shares the disenchantment of other social movements, NGOs and civil society organizations with a multilateral system that appears to have sold out to the forces of neo-liberalism dominated by the policy choices of Europe and North America. Nevertheless, with all its limitations and contradictions, the UN remains the only forum in which a global women's movement might engage governments in relation to agendas in which they are heavily invested. The adoption of the Millennium Development Goals (MDGs), with all their limitations,[23] provides a new focus for women's activism within the UN. For this reason, the UN's current initiative to examine its relations with civil society is welcome, although past experience would argue for extreme caution as the movement continues its engagement with this institution. In particular, NGOs need to be wary of the UN's initiative for 'partnership' with NGOs. As DAWN points out:

> The Partnerships Initiatives lock NGOs into a very difficult position. On the one hand, they provide opportunity to engage in dialogue … On the other, they represent a strategy of control and deliberately gloss over the inequalities in power and capacity of different actors (NGOs and TNCs); and use NGO participation to legitimize the claims to democracy in the neo-liberal models of governance.[24]

At the same time, the global women's movement must remain aware of its own limitations in relation to its capacity to ensure the implementation of these agendas at local levels. Indeed, a global women's movement can only provide frameworks whose effectiveness depends on the capacity, or willingness, of local women's movements to make them part of local struggles. The global women's movement must continue to recognize the crucial importance of these local links if the achievements of the 1990s are to survive in the less enabling environment of the new century.

Whether the efforts of women's movements in the past twenty-five years of activism translate into effective action for change requires a critical assessment of the strategies that women's movements have used in this period of time. The next two chapters will examine the complexities, tensions, contradictions, flaws and limitations of the global women's movement, and its efforts to transform the relationship and structures that perpetuate poverty, violence and exclusion.

Notes

1 Best-known publications: Vandana Shiva (1992) *Staying Alive: Women, Ecology and Development*, London: Zed Books; Rosalie Bertell (1985) *No Immediate Danger: Prognosis for a Radioactive Earth*, London: The Women's Press; Marilyn Waring (1952) *If Women Counted: A New Feminist Economics*, San Francisco: Harper & Row.

2 The Round had been launched in 1986 to review the General Agreement of Trade and Tariffs (GATT), with a view to replacing it with a new, enforceable agreement. The Round was to lead to the establishment of the World Trade Organization.

3 Marilyn Waring had earlier concluded that the chief beneficiaries of the agreements reached at the Earth Summit would be economists and lawyers.

4 One of the most significant differences being the inclusion in the Women's Agenda of paragraphs critical of the proposed trade agreements. Officials negotiating Agenda 21 regarded trade as off limits.

5. See DAWN's platform document for this conference, *Challenging the Given* (website details p. 189).

6 Recent work by Amartya Sen and UNHRC recognizes the link between poverty reduction and human rights, including women's human rights, and that these are not separate projects, but mutually reinforcing approaches to the same project.

7 DAWN's platform document, *Markers on the Way*, argues that

women have a primary role to play in public decision-making since they stand at the crossroads of economic growth and social development and therefore have most at stake when the two work at cross purposes.

8 Maria Suares Jaro (2000) *Women's Voices on Fire*, p. 116.

9 The international Human Rights Tribune credited the women's campaign with contributing to publicity for the conference in general, and with forcing UN member states to put the item on the agenda of the conference.

10 The concept of structural violence allows us to understand violence in the widest context of structures that serve to justify, reinforce and perpetuate violence against women and children. Violence is psychological, economic and political as well as physical. The mere threat of violence is sufficient to keep women in line.

11 As early as 1985 at the NGO Forum in Nairobi, the Vatican's representatives had tried to make common cause with Third World women who were critical of coercive and dangerous family planning programmes.

12 Correa and Reichman (1994); see Bibliography.

13 It helped that the US administration at that time was fully in support of women's rights.

14 A group of that name, HERA, was established under the leadership of the International Women's Health Coalition (IWHC) and DAWN to promote and monitor the Programme of Action.

15 By 2000, the US administration had changed to one controlled by the religious right, and this served to reinforce the efforts of the Vatican and Muslim fundamentalists.

16 Sen and Correa, *DAWN Informs* (2000) (see DAWN website).

17 DAWN's analysis of the politics surrounding the five-year reviews has been critical in helping the women's movement understand the context in which these negotiations were taking place, and helped focus lobbying and advocacy efforts.

18 A number of feminists are working on these linkages.

19 Viviene Taylor is DAWN's Research Coordinator on the theme of 'Political Restructuring and Social Transformation'; see Taylor (2000) and *DAWN Informs* (1998) 2, p. 8.

20 A concept used by DAWN in its platform document for the five-year review of the World Summit on Social Development, which captures the switch in orientation of the state away from the needs of citizens to those of the market.

21 See the declaration drawn up by the Women's International

Coalition for Economic Justice (WICEJ) on the eve of the five-year review of the 1995 conference (website www.wicej.org).

22. Wolte (in Braig and Wolte, 2002), p. 172.

23 See my critique on the MDGs – 'The Most Distracting Gimmick' – on the DAWN website.

24 *DAWN Informs*, May 2002, p. 8.

7 | Political strategies and dynamics of women's organizing and feminist activism

Women engaged in organizing and acting for change regarding the conditions and position of women employ a variety of strategies that range from reformist to revolutionary. All strategies may be valid in specific circumstances and for particular purposes. This chapter looks critically at the political strategies and political dynamics of women's organizations and feminist activism in organizing for change towards a more equitable and humane world. In analysing these strategies, I consider the lessons learned from the experience of the 1990s, and identify some of the tensions, shortcomings and limitations of the global movement.

I shall argue that, despite limitations, the strategies used by women in their organizing offer new and more varied possibilities for effective action. I will also argue that these forms of organizing draw strength from, and are specifically related to, the feminist politics and praxis used by leadership, and that this leadership is key to the achievement of the goals of women's movements.

Although I divide the strategies into three categories, activist, institutional and crosscutting, they often overlap, or get applied at different stages of struggles. In the first category I would list consciousness-raising groups, women's circles, coalition and alliance-building, global conferences and campaigns. In the second, research, analysis and advocacy, mainstreaming, monitoring and accountability. In the third, analysis, advocacy and networking, that cuts across the other two, often linking them.

Activist strategies

In my own analysis of women's organizing I have identified six 'spaces': consciousness-raising groups, women's circles, caucuses, coalitions, conferences and campaigns. I sometimes think of these as forming a continuum starting with the smallest most intimate group and extending to the mass campaign. Like a pebble dropped in water, the individual experience extends to progressively larger circles, incorporating, or being incorporated by, increasing diversity, until in the campaign the individual may find herself part of a mass movement of people who often have conflicting interests.

Consciousness-raising groups Feminist consciousness-raising is an important first step towards the identification and 'naming' of female subordination. Without this, activism can remain abstract, a purely intellectual notion of 'oppression' that fails to translate into lived experience and serious commitment to challenge female subordination. Although consciousness-raising is associated with 'white, middle-class housewives' in North America and Europe, it is far more widespread than that; for example, it was the basis of the 'speak bitterness' campaigns in China, out of which emerged challenges to foot binding and concubinage.

Consciousness-raising is experiential learning: through reflection on the personal experience of gender-based oppression, women can gain a deeper understanding of the experience of other forms of oppression based on class, race, ethnicity, culture and international relations. The process of consciousness-raising is an important tool in feminist organizing: making the link between one's own experience and the experience of others based on other categories of exclusion can be a powerful analytical tool, a stimulus to action that benefits oneself and others. Indeed, it is precisely because women of every class, race, ethnic group and country can identify with the experience of structured exclusion, marginalization and alienation within patriarchal society, that they can identify with the exclusion, marginalization and alienation of others on the basis of class, race/ethnicity, culture, religion, geographic location, age, physical ability, etc.

In the 1960s, breaking the silence of bourgeois and marital 'respectability', middle-class women shared experiences of oppression, exclusion and alienation to discover that they were not alone. This generated the analysis, consciousness and energy necessary to make change in their own lives. Many went on to become active in the women's liberation movement. However, what was lacking in this process, for women from North America and Europe, was an analysis of the links to other forms of oppression. A more holistic analysis of the links between the multi-layered sources of women's oppression in specific situations can help strengthen women's movements in their search for justice for everyone. In this way, identity politics can lead to the larger feminist social project.

Women's circles Women's circles are the spaces in which most organizing starts. The circle is made up of a group of close friends or colleagues, who share a common political philosophy and agenda. Women engaged in political action in the area of social change towards gender justice need a safe space with like-minded sisters in which to hone their analysis and develop strategies; a space in which there is sufficient trust to encourage honesty and critical thinking.[1] These small groups may be formalized as committees or working groups, meeting on an on-going basis to analyse and strategize. They may also be ad hoc, formed as caucuses within the context of conferences or campaigns.

Caucuses The women's caucuses initiated by WEDO within the framework of UN conferences have become institutionalized. Although the analysis of options that informs the positions taken and strategies used by women at these conferences is often formulated in informal meetings of feminists (women's circles), the women's caucuses are the public spaces in which strategies for lobbying governments are negotiated. Under the leadership[2] of WEDO, women participating in UN conferences developed caucusing to a fine art, expanding the space for NGOs at the UN.

Preparations for the women's caucus included detailed analysis of conference documents and the drafting of amendments to the texts. Throughout the 1990s, WEDO circulated these documents to partner networks and individual women. At the same time, other networks, such as those on women's human rights and DAWN, would be involved in their own preparatory analyses of the documents as well as of the political context for the negotiations. Meetings of preparatory committees, PrepComs, provided opportunities for refining and testing alternative texts and, most importantly, for assessing allies and antagonists.

Women's caucuses are now a standard part of most international meetings, and are spaces in which newcomers and individual women can link their lobbying efforts to those more experienced in these activities. They are also unparalleled spaces for education, analysis, solidarity and movement building.

Coalition and alliance building Coalition and alliance building (national, regional, global/North–South, within and outside the movement) has been an important strategy for the global movement. The understanding of the linkages between the social, political, economic and cultural concerns of women, along with an analysis that links women's experience at the personal and micro level of the community to the common policy framework of neo-liberalism, has facilitated and encouraged the formation of alliances and coalitions, as shown in Chapter 6. For this reason, there has been more coherence and convergence in women's organizing than in that of other social movements. For example, during the conferences of the 1990s, women's networks concerned with the environment worked with those concerned with population, reproductive rights and development. The 'networking of networks' that was noted at the second World Social Forum in Porto Alegre (2002) was pioneered, tested and honed by women's movements at local and global levels during the global conferences of the 1990s.

Coalitions and alliances may be formed with other women's networks, as well as with NGOs working on common issues. However, while coalition and alliance building between women's groups and networks enriches the alliance or coalition by broadening the scope of the analysis and advocacy, that between women and other NGOs brings a perspective which may entail complex negotiations of the differences between the parties before the alliance or coalition can be effective in carrying out the task for which it was formed.

As DAWN has found in its work on environmental issues,

women's perspectives can often be very different from those of NGOs, even those NGOs in which there are large numbers of women. An analysis that starts from the daily experience of poor women is one that rejects dualisms of personal and political, private and public, etc. A good example of this was given in the previous chapter in relation to DAWN's analysis on the environment. Mainstream environmental groups seldom start from this place, nor do they give the attention that feminists do to the links between women's needs and concerns and those expressed in their advocacy.

On the other hand, alliances and coalitions between women's networks have enriched advocacy and expanded outreach. Thus the women's human rights networks have linked with women's networks on reproductive health, or on economic issues, in order to underscore the indivisibility of women's human rights and emphasize the interconnectedness of the civil, political, social, economic and cultural dimensions of all human rights.

The use of women's experiences as a starting point for analysis is what makes the difference between the work of women in mainstream NGOs (where women's ideas and experiences are often marginalized) and their work with other women. The adoption of this starting point is basically an adaptation of the methodology of consciousness-raising.

Global conferences:
UN CONFERENCES A great deal has been said about UN conferences in Chapters 4 and 6. I include them here to complete the list, to make some general observations, and specifically to consider the UN conference as a strategy for facilitating consensus at the global level around international norms, standards and accountability.

Global conferences have provided an important space for women's organizing, linking the work of movements at local levels to that at the global level. But what is often missed, when the spotlight is shone on the global arena, is the amount of preparatory work that goes into it. Indeed, without this preparatory work at local level, and again within the caucuses formed around

The purposes served by UN conferences

I can think of three; there are undoubtedly more.

Educational. There is nothing like an international conference for raising awareness, generating knowledge and developing skills in advocacy, lobbying and negotiating. Many of the educational experiences take place on the fringe of the conference, in the panels and workshops organized by conference organizers, NGOs and women's organizations on related topics, and in the caucuses and corridors as much as in the conference rooms. Perhaps more in these other spaces than in the conference rooms, where official propaganda and geo-political considerations often prevail.

Political. Conferences provide opportunities for negotiating the international norms and standards that set the framework for negotiation at local levels and for holding governments and international agencies accountable. They also provide unique opportunities for the networking, alliance and coalition building that create political capital for the movements.

Social. The social aspects of movement building cannot be ignored. Effective political action depends on good interpersonal relations and trust. The relationships developed and reinforced by the series of UN conferences spanning over thirty-five years have made it possible for women to continue to work together on movement building. Conferences build the social capital without which political action cannot be sustained.

the arena of global events, global conferences are little more than theatre. UN conferences are clearly unparalleled in the opportunities they provide for education, networking and movement building. Without them it is difficult to imagine how a global women's movement might have emerged, or manifested itself.

UN conferences have served women well, but they have also been frustrating experiences for many activists. The formality of these intergovernmental meetings, the often meaningless rhetoric, and the dynamic of political forces and geopolitical realities that often have little to do with the issues at hand, have led many women to question their value beyond a certain point. For the global women's movement they have been the arena in which great gains have been made in terms of articulating and advancing women's agendas, but they have also been spaces in which women have had to contend with the political realities of North–South divisions and the manipulations of fundamentalist forces, as well as with the failure of their governments to honour commitments and agreements made in their own countries.

Increasingly, women engaged in these conferences have faced criticism from colleagues in the movement over the amount of time spent in these spaces against the needs of local movements, as well as in relation to the limited impact that international agreements have at local level in many instances. After all these years of UN meetings and events, women are questioning the value of further conferences. In the first instance, many women feel that there are enough programmes and platforms of action, resolutions and mandates to provide a basis for all the work that can be undertaken for decades to come: action on implementation, rather than more words, is what is required at this stage.

In addition to this, in recent years, with the strengthening of the fundamentalist backlash against women's advancement, women have had to struggle to maintain the ground gained in previous UN conferences. The five-year reviews of the ICPD and the Beijing conference have shown that UN conferences also provide opportunities for manoeuvre by forces opposed to women's advancement in order to reverse hard-won gains.

There is currently a debate about the value of holding another World Conference on Women in 2005.[3] This conference was proposed as an occasion for noting progress on the implementation of the programme of action from the Fourth World Conference, but the current views of some women's organizations and networks and the withdrawal of certain critical networks from the process make it unlikely, although there will be a CSW review of the Beijing Platform in 2005.

Political strategies

Despite these concerns, there is no doubt about the value of conferences for networking and for expanding the movements at local and global levels. My own assessment is that, while the UN remains an important space for interacting with governments and the UN system itself, and for educational purposes, its political importance for women and for other social movements is lessened as it forms closer alliances with the IFIs and the corporate sector. It should be abundantly clear by this time that the UN is unlikely to do the kind of sharp analysis and critique of the neo-liberal agenda that would give hope for change. Without an analysis that acknowledges the extent to which the power imbalance inherent in neo-liberalism stands as an obstacle to the achievement of the laudable goals of UN conferences, there is no basis for hope that these will be achieved.

OTHER (NON-UN) CONFERENCES Women have their own conferences. Before, and beyond, the UN Decade for Women, women from around the world had met around a variety of issues related to their rights. Among the major international women's conferences today are those organized by the Association for Women's Rights and Development (AWID) and the Women's International Inter-discipline Congress. While they do not have the resources and visibility of UN conferences, they provide opportunities for women to meet around their own agendas, produce clearer analyses and strengthen their movements.

Beyond women's conferences is the World Social Forum (WSF), the meeting place of the new social movement for global justice. Since its inception in 2000, this movement has been gaining in strength and visibility, fuelled by the continuing injustices of North–South relations, the collusion of international institutions in this, and corporate-led globalization. The WSF has now become the most important space for the mobilization of resistance to the relentless push for extension of the neo-liberal agenda. The global women's movement is part of this larger movement, although much more work needs to be done to realize any real partnership between the male-led organizations and networks and women's networks. In any event, beyond the mobilization against corporate-led globalization, and now the war in Iraq, and opportunities for networking, the campaigns of the movement for global justice, and the organization of the WSF itself, do not allow for the kind of communication and negotiations needed if the global women's movement is to have any real influence in these spaces. These issues will be addressed more fully in the next chapter.

Women's campaigns It can be argued that women's movements have achieved more from campaigns – especially those organized by networks with strong links between movements at local level and initiatives at global level – than they have from conferences. Particularly effective have been the global campaigns around women's human rights and against violence against women. However, campaigns around local issues have been easier to organize and more effective in achieving their objectives. Examples are the campaign against genital mutilation in parts of Africa, against dowry deaths in India, for the extension of reproductive rights in parts of Latin America, and, of course, the ongoing campaign against violence against women.

A good example of a global campaign is the Global Campaign for Women's Human Rights (GCWHR), referred to in Chapter 6 (see also below). Of special note here are the role played by other spaces – the women's circle and the caucus – and the importance of coalition building as well. The strategic planning institute in support of the GCWHR was in a sense a 'women's circle' which facilitated the formulation of strategies for linking the daily experiences of women at local levels to the global campaign.

Conclusions on activist strategies I want to end this section by commenting on the unevenness of the experience of women's organizing over the past twenty-five years. Although these comments relate to the strategies of local movements rather than to the global movement, they remind us of the diversity of the local experiences in which the global is grounded.

• Despite the range of issues around which women have organ-

What is the Global Campaign for Women's Human Rights?

The GCWHR is a loose coalition of groups and individuals worldwide, formed in preparation for the UN Conference on Human Rights held in Vienna in 1993. Since the initial call for the conference did not mention women or recognize any gender-specific aspects of human rights in its proposed agenda, this became a natural vehicle for women's activities. One of the early actions of the campaign was a petition launched in 1991 that called on the Vienna conference to 'comprehensively address women's human rights at every level of its proceedings' and recognize 'gender violence, a universal phenomenon which takes many forms across culture, race, and class ... as a violation of human right requiring immediate action'. A global leadership petition, distributed by the Center for Women's Global Leadership (CWGL) and the International Women's Tribune Centre (IWTC), was circulated through dozens of women's networks and taken up by women at all levels to further their organizing efforts. The petition had been launched at the first annual campaign of Sixteen Days of Activism Against Gender Violence, a global umbrella for local activities that promote public awareness about gender-based violence as a human rights concern. Groups participating in the campaign select their own objectives and determine their own local activities, within a larger global effort with some common themes. The campaign grew steadily during the 1990s, involving groups in over a hundred countries in

ized over the past twenty-five years, the *most effective organizing* has occurred around issues relating to violence against women, sexual and reproductive health and rights, and livelihood/ environmental issues such as access to land, forests and water. These are issues that link gender justice to economic justice.
• Although the women's movement has been active, in alliances and coalitions with other social movements and groups, in

events including hearings, demonstrations, media campaigns, cultural festivals and candlelight vigils. Many of its activities also mobilized women to participate in the UN world conferences. Since 1995, it has campaigned for implementation of the promises made to women in the various conference documents as well as in UN treaties such as the Convention on the Elimination of All Forms of Discrimination Against Women (CEDAW). The success of the global campaign was rooted in the activities of national and regional women's groups, who defined the important issues in their countries as they focused attention on the world conferences.

As part of this process CWGL held a strategic planning institute to coordinate plans for Vienna with women from around the world who had been active regionally. This meeting, in Geneva in April 1993, worked on lobbying strategies for the conference, including further development of recommendations on women's human rights; built on regional proposals, and served as the final international preparatory meeting. Institute attendees also began preparations for a Global Tribunal on Violations of Women's Human Rights that would give vivid personal expression to the consequences of such violations. Participants would provide graphic demonstration of how being female can be life-threatening, discussing such abuses as torture, terrorism and slavery, connecting human rights abuse in the family, war crimes against women, violations of women's bodily integrity, socio-economic violations, and political persecution and discrimination.[4]

organizing efforts around citizenship and constitutional change (Latin America, South Africa, Fiji); structural adjustment and debt (Latin America, Africa, the Caribbean); poverty and landlessness (Asia); militarism (Pacific), it has been *less successful* in having its specific, gendered issues addressed in these broader struggles.

- Women's activism has been *stronger in some regions and countries* than in others. For example, the women's movement in the Caribbean seems dormant when compared with that in Latin America. However, differences in culture and political structures determine the nature of women's organizing at local level.

- Although organizing at the global level is important in terms of setting international standards and programmes of action, meaningful changes in women's lives depend on the extent to which these are translated into *local organizing*.

At the same time there are paradoxes that caution against reaching simple conclusions. Here are a few.

- Within the Caribbean some of the best examples of policies that come closest to women's agendas in the areas of health (including abortion), education, civil rights and economic empowerment occur in a country (Barbados) where the movement is *apparently weak* (especially when compared with other countries such as Jamaica and Trinidad).
- In some countries, *the church and the family* represent spaces from which women draw strength. It has been noted that in Czechoslovakia, especially during communism, the family was indeed one of the spaces within which women experienced a measure of liberation. In the Caribbean also, where the patriarchal family is weak, the family and the household constitute such a space: the extended family tends to include a number of independent women, and this is a major source of support for women and children, especially for women without male support.
- In the base communities of Latin America, the *Roman Catholic Church* showed that it could be a *liberating force* for women; many women find their faith a source of strength and empowerment.
- In countries without democratic institutions, or where women's rights are curtailed, *global action* may be the most effective means of guaranteeing women's rights or security at local level.

Where is the rage? There is another issue to be addressed before moving on to consider institutional strategies, and that is the criticism that women's movements have lost their political edge. I think this sometimes comes from judging women's movements by the expectations of models of left-wing politics. The issue might be posed this way: there is passion in this movement, but where is the rage? Women's revolutionary action seems to be different from that of men, grounded in a socialization that constructs women as less violent, more accommodating, than men. However, although women's political activism may be less violent than that of their brothers in struggle, their actions are no less revolutionary. How else does one describe a campaign to stop men who beat women by picketing their homes, or to get men to support their children by shaming them in their work-place, or to stop bulldozers by hugging trees, or confront the military by daily marches in the public square?

These strategies are designed for very specific locations. At the global level the protests rely on linking struggles around the world, from International Women's Day (8 March) to the Sixteen Days Against Gender Violence (10–25 November). They also rely on campaigns and symbols that are outrageous, like the campaign led by Latin American women at the most recent World Social Forum (2003), against 'fundamentalisms ... all of them' – a campaign that juxtaposes pictures of Bush, Bin Laden, Saddam Hussein and the Pope.

The strengthening of women's movements in the 1980s in the context of the UN Decade for Women, the opening up of democratic space in the countries of Latin America and mobilizations there around feminist critiques of IMF-inspired structural adjustment policies, the triumph of neo-liberalism in the 1990s, and globalization since the mid-1990s, have opened the way to what some have termed *discursive democracy* – a concept that champions an active and informed citizenry, engaged in policy discourse to challenge and seek change in the status quo. While this engagement with policy-making processes has also carried the risk of co-optation,[5] it would be fair to say that the gains in terms of democracy have been considerable. Engagement in UN debates, as well as in those on debt and structural adjustment and globalization, have made women at all levels more knowledgeable about the political economy of neo-liberalism, a subject to which women had not paid much attention hitherto.

As we seek transformations of power, the most revolutionary approach for women's movements may be to reject male definitions of power and revolution.

Institutional strategies

Since the 1990s, within the processes of the global conferences, the emerging global women's movement has created links between public discourse – which takes place in civil society – and the policy discourse that takes place among technocrats and political elites within systems of governance. Local women's movements linked to a global movement have engaged in policy dialogues, often without sacrificing their political legitimacy. It was through interaction between feminist activists (experts in their own right) and mainstream 'experts' (who may also be feminists) that activists often changed the terms of the debate on issues like human rights and reproductive rights. This also led to more direct engagement of feminist activists in bureaucratic processes such as mainstreaming and monitoring government policies and programmes to ensure accountability.

Mainstreaming The strategy of mainstreaming – integrating new frameworks, agendas, findings and strategies into mainstream policies, programmes and projects – has been used increasingly for advancing women's concerns. Institutions that have set up special programmes for women, or adopted UN mandates, especially favour this strategy. The Women/Gender and Development (W/GD) programmes of UN agencies, the World Bank, and bilateral aid agencies, have all supported mainstreaming. Some women's organizations and activist networks have also adopted mainstreaming strategies as they focus on the implementation of the various plans and programmes of action.

However, the effectiveness of this strategy has been mixed. Working to mainstream women's concerns leads inevitably to a degree of bureaucratization that depoliticizes, and can therefore weaken the effectiveness of the effort. Mainstreaming can, perhaps, be most effective when combined with mechanisms for independent monitoring by political groups working outside the institutions concerned.[6] At worst, it can lead to the disappearance of the focus on women, rendering them once again 'invisible', and distract from contradictory policies, covering up the absence of real change and a lack of political will. In instances where rhetoric about 'gender equity' becomes a tool of public relations, it can lead to justifiable cynicism.

For example, the gender mainstreaming strategies of many multilateral agencies, such as the UN and the World Bank, as well as bilateral aid agencies, include impressive gender assessment checklists, guidelines and gender impact assessments to be applied to all programmes and policies. However, these are often contradicted by policy frameworks that undermine and jeopardize the goals, objectives and values of the strategies. Thus the World Bank's Country Gender Assessment is intended

> to be used in dialogue with borrower governments to identify priority gender-responsive policies and interventions in high-impact sectors important for poverty reduction, economic growth and sustainable development [and in] the reform of institutions to establish equal rights and opportunities for women and men; fostering economic development to strengthen incentives for more equal resources and participation; and taking active measures to redress persistent disparities in command over resources and political voice.

But the Bank continues to push policies which directly contradict these laudable objectives. The fundamental contradiction between policies that favour the interests of multinational corporations and those that favour the poor and marginalized has yet to be addressed by international institutions. Many activists are therefore justifiably critical of mainstreaming policies that deny political realities, and many from the global women's movement have come away from interactions with these institutions with feelings of disappointment and betrayal. When it comes to issues of gender equity, the limitations of purely 'technical-professional' approaches are all too clear.

Monitoring and accountability In the wake of UN conferences, monitoring governments and other institutions and holding them to account for the implementation of resolutions, recommendations and international conventions have become important strategies for change. Having fought for these provisions in international fora, feminist activists at local levels have tried to use them to legitimize and give strength to their advocacy. However, it is important to recognize that, in many cases, governments sign on to resolutions, programmes of action and even conventions that they have no intention of implementing. Feminist activists understand this and know that while international instruments provide political and normative guidelines, they must be 'domesticated' – translated into local realities and made meaningful to local movements – if they are to be meaningful for women in the country. Feminist activists have given a great deal of thought to how this might be done, and some interesting mechanisms have been devised.[7]

Crosscutting strategies

Research, analysis and advocacy From the mid-1970s, research has been an important strategy for the movement. As mentioned in Chapter 4, the research generated by the UN Decade for Women served to make women's realities visible, while also revealing the links between the social relations of gender and the political, economic, social and cultural structures that marginalize and jeopardize whole communities and groups of people. Research and analysis have been the basis of advocacy, which to some extent has been effective in changing laws as well as some practices and attitudes.

However, postmodernist scholars and others have challenged the research on 'Third World women' carried out early in the Decade for Women. They argue, with some truth, that there was a tendency to present 'Third World women' as a category, a homogeneous 'powerless' group often located as implicit victims of particular socio-economic systems. This would be a fair criticism of research on women from Third World countries that denied the specificity of the varied and complex experiences of women in these countries. This is particularly important if research is to form the basis for policy change or direct political action, especially action by groups marginalized by race/ethnicity, class and location. However, starting with the challenge by African researchers in the African Association for Women and Development at the end of the 1970s to Western hegemony in the area of research on women, many scholar-activists have corrected this shortcoming, and in the process have produced a body of work that has informed political strategies and shaped advocacy since the mid-1980s. Following the path set by DAWN, the analysis produced by many global women's networks today is built on the differences between women of different regions, cultures, political orientations, racial and ethnic groups. Moreover, efforts are made to present an analysis 'from the perspective of the most marginalized groups', even if the researchers are not representative of this class or race.

In terms of political strategy it might be useful to distinguish between research and analysis that has supported reform and that which suggests the need for more radical change. The keys to differences in research methodologies and findings have been the theoretical and conceptual frameworks used, and the purpose for which the research is produced. These determine not only the questions asked but the relationships between different data sets. We have seen the same researcher produce very different analyses and conclusions according to the frameworks used. Thus, research and analysis carried out by Third World scholars like those involved in the DAWN collective can be contrasted with that carried out by scholars from similar backgrounds, as individuals, for institutions such as the World Bank, the UN and even independent research centres.

There is also a better understanding of the distinction to be made between research carried out for the purpose of advocacy and that carried out for the purpose of scholarship. When research is linked to advocacy, or policy, the questions must be determined by the needs of those who would use the research.[8]

In many instances research has been central to raising awareness, a process critical for launching or strengthening women's organizing. In many countries, commissions on the status of women led to institutional change, while research centres and women's studies programmes within the academy made important contributions to the promotion of feminist perspectives or the sensitization of the state to women's concerns.

Another important distinction must be made between different methodologies. It is fairly well accepted now that participatory methodologies are most appropriate for research intended to produce social change. Here the research process is as important as the output. Indeed, the gap between research and action can be reduced considerably by the use of participatory methodologies, which generate new knowledge as well as new consciousness of the contradictions and social relations of power; both are required for the promotion of social change.

Networking Networking has been one of the commonest strategies used by women's movements at all levels. It might be said that it is through networking that the global women's movement emerged: networking brought women together in formal and informal ways, around conferences and campaigns and outside these spaces, and helped the process of discovering 'common differences' on which solidarity was built.

Since 1975, and in the context of the UN Decade for Women, a number of women's networks emerged at all levels – local, national, regional and international (see list on pp. 189–90). Some have focused on single issues or specific activities; others are more general. The global women's movement, as represented by these networks, might also be conceptualized as an on-going campaign for women's rights and empowerment.

Approaches to social change

In relation to women's organizing for change, it is useful to think of a 'typology of social change efforts based on an analysis of their divergent root assumptions about value and the nature of reality rather than a categorization of their various activities'.[9] Three perspectives of social change can be identified: the professional-technical, the political and the counter-cultural, each leading to different strategies, methodologies and types of leadership. While it is clear, as is the case with all attempts at categorizing, that reality is more complex than theoretical formulations suggest, making distinctions between different perspectives and understanding their association with different paradigms help us analyse the different approaches used by the global women's movement and aid our understanding of what is needed if this movement is to contribute to the movement for global justice.

The global ideological and policy framework is presently dominated by professional-technical perspectives. Given the concentration of power in the hands of a global elite, there seems little chance that this approach, by itself, can achieve either broad-based socio-economic improvement for the majority, or the more specific goals embodied in the women's agendas negotiated at various UN conferences. Women's movements have, by definition, used the political approach. However, what has been significant, in the context of the global conferences, is the way in which traditional political approaches have been combined with professional-technical approaches. I would argue that what is needed now is some greater, more explicit, integration of counter-cultural[10] approaches with the professional-technical and political approaches adopted by the global women's movement to date.

To be sure, there are women and women's groups who have used a counter-cultural approach in their organizing,[11] especially at local levels. Some are part of the global women's movement as I have defined it. They may be largely marginalized, and yet they have a great deal to offer the more politically oriented movement. At the same time, for these counter-cultural groups, organizing autonomously, the adoption of professional-technical and political approaches could strengthen their efforts towards social change. At local levels it is particularly important for politically oriented women's movements to build alliances with these groups, since they enrich our understanding of a different kind of power – power within – a power that is often missing in mainstream women's movements, but one that is essential. In my view, all three are required for the changes that women seek, because of the systemic linkages between economic, social, cultural and political structures. But a counter-cultural approach is more than

Seven

Summarizing Chesler's and Crowfoot's approaches to social change

The *professional-technical* approach is ostensibly the conventional, mainstream approach to development and social change in Western democracies. It is based on the assumption that 'only a certain class (race and gender as well) has the intellectual expertise to make decisions for the rest of society. In general these are people, whether local or foreign, who have been educated according to the dominant ideology and who subscribe to its values and dictates. This kind of hegemony is the more difficult to break because it is backed up by an economic system which is strongly entrenched and reinforced by the benefits it brings to those in power and by the interdependence of social, cultural, political and economic relations and moral obligations' (p. 81).

This perspective falls within a paradigm, or world view, that considers society, and most of its organizations and institutions, to be basically sound, needing only to manage change better, to be more transparent, accountable, and less 'corrupt'.

The *political approach*, which recognizes the role power relations play in decision-making, may also go to the other extreme of denying the value of sound professional input in the change process. Nevertheless, it comes closer to reality and provides a better basis for planning strategies for change, especially in relation to women in patriarchal societies. The political approach acknowledges that society is made up of different groups 'each defined by the uniquely shared interests of its members, each with different and often competing interests or goals'. These groups may be based on race, ethnicity, class, gender or location, and there are usually imbalances of power between them and the dominant group.

Crowfoot and Chesler say, 'This approach recognises the inevitability of conflict between the groups since, when commodities such as material goods, information, technical skill, respect, status and so on are perceived as scarce, groups will compete for their control. This is where the state needs to intervene in order to guarantee an equitable distribution of goods and resources. However, if those who operate the apparatus of the state are themselves beneficiaries of the system they will tend to opt for stability rather than equality in regulating the relations among groups and between groups and resources. The result is a high concentration of power in the hands of a few people or a few interest groups ... The change process is initiated when this is understood and people are willing to deal with these differences in the interest of the common good' (pp. 83–4).

This approach accords with the 'conflict' or 'alternative' paradigm. It is not an approach that is often acknowledged by those in control. Yet failure to acknowledge that people of different classes, races, ethnic groups, genders and location etc. can have appreciably different interests from those in power may be the single most significant obstacle to change in today's world, where power is so concentrated in the hands of an international elite. This denial of the political imbalances and conflicting interests inherent in the assumptions underlying neo-liberal policy agendas, from those of structural adjustment to the trade agreements enforced by the WTO, explains the difficulties NGOs have had in making the case for global justice.

More importantly, this approach requires women's movements to pay more attention to issues of race/ethnicity, class and location.

The *counter-cultural approach* is the most neglected, but of critical importance for women and other marginalized groups. This approach is based on 'affirming the culture and values of the society. It is suspicious of over technocratic and over bureaucratic approaches and concepts of progress', since these are considered to lead to a marginalization of local or indigenous knowledge, a decrease of initiative, creativity and individuality, and to inhibiting the individual from realizing his or her full human potential. This perspective places emphasis on individual change – in personal values, life styles and relationships with others, and emphasizes communal organizations as the building and rebuilding blocks of a new unalienating society.

Adapted from Crowfoot and Chesler (1992)

one approach among three. Using a definition[12] of culture as 'the particular ways in which a social group lives out and makes sense of its "given" circumstances and conditions of life', or as a 'system through which ... a social order is communicated, reproduced, experienced and explored', we have recognized that those whose advocacy challenges norms and attitudes deeply embedded in patriarchal culture face a particularly difficult task.

During the past twenty-five years of advocacy on behalf of women's rights within the UN and other international agencies and institutions as well as at local level in relation to the state, the strongest resistance to change has been in relation to gender equity. Moreover, this is an area of advocacy that most states are unwilling to press on others: governments and international institutions have no difficulty pressing conditionalities in relation to economic and social policies, but when it comes to gender they hold back, talking about 'policies that are consistent with national laws and traditions'. Patriarchs do not challenge other patriarchs. VeneKlasen, quoted in Miller (2001), reinforces this:

It is not just the externally enforced social roles and expectations that perpetuate women's subordination and male superiority, it is the insidious way that culture shapes a man's psyche about 'proper' gender roles and the way it forms a woman's sense of self to ensure that she is often her best keeper. This is true in industrialized countries of the North – where the conflicting images of glamour and domestic nurturer set impossible standards for the ordinary woman to achieve – as much as it is true in nations of the South, where many woman cannot dream of leaving their home or participating in public life, let alone have aspirations for the future. The role that culture plays in perpetuating inferiority and the imbalance of power is profoundly political.

What this means is that women engaged in organizing for social change need a closer examination of power to assist in devising and selecting the strategies that might be most effective. Specifically, more attention has to be paid to the invisible power that operates to make advocacy on behalf of gender equity particularly difficult. This includes the internalization of 'the underlying ideology of female inferiority, which is disguised in an idealised image of women as perfect wife and mother'.[13]

Analysis of power

Advocacy on behalf of women's agency and rights is by definition political, yet many advocates for gender equity proceed on the assumption that the asymmetry of gender relations can be sidestepped. Too often advocacy addresses itself to power structures that are visible and formal, and takes the form of the presentation of 'rational' arguments. This ignores the fact that resistance is deeply embedded in the culture of patriarchy. To address this, other less traditional kinds of action are needed. A more careful analysis of power would provide clues to a wider range of strategies. As Foucault and others remind us, power is not monolithic, and is always subject to contestation. There are also different kinds of power – power over others, power with others, inner power, and power to do and act together. 'Power over' is what immediately comes to mind when one thinks of power. It is embodied in the visible power structure of the society – the state. Within institutions like the family, this kind of power is exercised by the head of the household – usually a man, but by women when they are in charge.

Writing about women's empowerment, some feminists (Batliwala and others) often emphasize the other types of power – power with, power within and power to act. These types of power 'expand the possibility to create more symmetrical, equitable relationships of power between and within people and groups and to foster human agency – the ability to act and change the world'.[14] Women's movements need to focus on these types of power, in addition to the more obvious power structure.

In addition, it is important to recognize that women, like men, have a range of identities and characteristics, and these can also be taken into account in determining strategies. Thus, while women who have a certain status and credibility within the power structure because of class, race/ethnicity, education, occupation, age and so on may have more success, they may also be constrained by these same factors from pursuing less 'acceptable' strategies. Solidarity among women activists can lead to a creative and effective mix of 'insider-outsider' strategies.

Solidarity among women across common divides of class, race/ethnicity, etc., allows them to draw on the power of collective action – 'power with' – that can be effective precisely because of the diversity of those involved. This is a particular strength of women's movements, and more attention needs to be paid to it.

An even more important source of power is 'power within'. A few years ago, in a discussion about 'empowerment' (sources of power), grassroots women in the Caribbean mentioned spirituality and sexuality. They made it clear that they were not referring to either religion (which they described as 'disempowering'), or sexual activity (which they felt could be distracting or oppressive). Spirituality and sexuality are sources of power that lie deep within women and are not frequently discussed. A counter-cultural approach would validate these sources of power. Women's circles and consciousness-raising processes provide spaces for this and should be recognized as important elements in women's organizing.

When confronting the formal power structure, women activists, especially those who are labelled 'feminist', need to recognize that they face a particular kind of resistance, which is cultural. The fact that the man or woman an activist is addressing does not acknowledge this simply underlines the power of patriarchy. The advocate assumes the person she is addressing is 'rational' and can be persuaded by the strength of her data and the logic of her argument. She needs to understand that this is far from the case. In the first instance because she is female, second because she is feminist, and third because of the nature of her advocacy, her advocacy is seldom taken seriously. Her presence, her politics and the content of her advocacy are all mediated by the culture of the person she is addressing. To this person she is 'unrealistic', 'illogical', 'irrational', 'hysterical', 'dangerous' – all because she dares to question the underlying assumptions of patriarchal culture. In this context, the nurturing of 'power within' to strengthen women's power to take action is critically important.

Equally important is that women who dare to act on behalf of women's agency be supported by others. Collective action by women from a variety of backgrounds can be powerful indeed. These kinds of power draw on the particular strengths of women's movements; I define these as counter-cultural approaches – countering the culture of patriarchy.

Lessons learned

Reflecting on the strategies used by the global women's movement in the past thirty years, I would underline the following lessons.

- *The most effective strategies are those that combine political with professional and counter-cultural approaches*, i.e. paying attention to *cultural* elements through spiritual growth, consciousness-raising/conscientization, solidarity and networking; political elements such as lobbying, advocacy, caucusing, coalition-alliance building including using insider/outsider approaches; and technical-professional elements i.e. sound research and analysis.
- *Multiple strategies are often necessary*. These include the following:
- *insider/outsider approaches*: critical engagement with the state while being accountable to the women's movement;
- *between sectors*: e.g. health, education and women's/gender

affairs in relation to HIV-AIDS, or health, welfare, housing and legal affairs in relation to domestic violence – in each case with links to women's movements;

- linking local to global: although some strategies may have been initiated at the global level, organizing must ultimately return to the *local level* if change is to be meaningful to women in these countries. Similarly, the most effective organizing at global level has been that which links with efforts at local level;

- *at local level*, strategies that link literacy or popular education with research and advocacy, in a dynamic interplay, have the most meaning for the grassroots and are the most likely to lead to empowerment and change in democratic societies;

- *research methodologies must be appropriate to the task*: if the purpose of the research is to inform advocacy, the key questions must be generated by activists, not researchers; if the purpose is empowerment, the methodology must be participatory;

- advocacy must be based on *sound research and analysis, and grounded in women's realities*;

- *advocacy is more difficult when powerful interests are threatened*, be they economic, political or ideological; therefore it must be informed by a *more careful analysis of power*: an understanding of the difference between visible power and invisible power, and the role of ideology in disempowering women;

- *alliances must be built with those mainstream NGOs that share the values of social justice*. However, we must start with leadership that acknowledges the importance of gender equity, winning allies before attempting to influence the larger group. This involves identifying and making alliances with men who are supportive of feminist leadership. Change for women requires change in the behaviour of men, and we need to recognize that there are men who identify with our agenda and see feminist analysis and women's agency as keys to the kind of personal and social transformation required to bring about the 'better' world they too seek. At the same time, however ...

- *alliance and coalition building must start with women* before reaching out to the wider civil society, otherwise women advocating change may find themselves isolated from or de-legitimized by other associations of women.

• *Feminist leadership is key.*

Conclusion

Women have used multiple strategies in their organizing, often reflecting regional and national differences in relation to the nature of the state, the strengths and weaknesses of the movement and the issues of concern to women at that particular time and context. I turn now to some of the challenges facing women's movements in general, and the global women's movement in particular, if they are to be more effective in their advocacy in the future.

Notes

1 In a sense, the steering committees or global networks like DAWN, the WICEJ, etc., are spaces where this kind of work takes place at a global level.

2 Under the leadership of the charismatic former US congresswoman, Bella Abzug, WEDO was established in the context of the preparations for UNCED. It later carved a niche for itself at the UN as the convenor of an increasingly effective women's caucus throughout the UN conferences of the 1990s.

3 See discussions on the websites of AWID, DAWN, and the proceedings of the 2003–04 Commission on the Status of Women.

4 Bunch and Reilly (1994).

5 A current (2004) example of this is in Haiti, where a wide range of civil society organizations have mobilized to oust the democratically elected President. I discuss this in greater detail in the Epilogue.

6 An example of this is the provision made by the Division for the Advancement of Women for independent reports on the implementation of CEDAW.

7 Brazil, for instance, has developed a framework for monitoring the implementation of the Programme of Action from ICPD.

8 In the International Gender and Trade Network this is well understood. Of course, as in the case of DAWN, the involvement of women who are both researchers and activists helps.

9 J. E. Crowfoot and M. A. Chesler (1974) 'Contemporary

Perspectives on Planned Social Change: A Comparison', *Journal of Applied Behavioural Science*, 10 (3), pp. 278–303.

10 Alda Facio argues for the creation of a feminist counter-culture 'from the arts, technologies, sciences, languages, symbols and myths from our true internal selves in connection with all other beings'. Her argument for a feminist spirituality and the use of consciousness-raising towards a feminist 'ultra-consciousness' (as distinct from a feminist consciousness) also resonate with my views expressed here and in Chapter 9. 'A feminist ultra-consciousness would allow us not only to see sexism in societal structures but also how sexism operates within us and how it is linked to all other forms of oppression.' See her chapter in Kerr et al. (2004) .

11 These would include women's movements that focus on spirituality or the Goddess or Mother Nature. See chapter by Alda Facio cited above.

12 Quoted in Miller (2001).

13 Oxfam UK, quoted in Miller (2001), p. 3.

14 Quoted in Miller (2001), pp. 4–5.

8 | The new context: challenges and dilemmas for the future

The relevance of a social movement must be judged in relation to the context in which it operates, as well as to its reach and effectiveness. The central question that this book attempts to answer is: Given the interlinked crises in social reproduction, human security and governance, and given that women are key stakeholders in these areas, what can the global women's movement contribute, through the larger movement for global justice, to finding solutions to these problems? This question must be answered in the context of the present conjuncture and the risks it holds for women and for those for whom they bear special responsibility.

At the start of this new millennium the context has changed dramatically from the second half of the 20th century. The present conjuncture is one that poses enormous risks to women and their loved ones. At the same time the institutional environment in which women's movements are operating has also become more problematic: the encouragement and opening up of spaces for women's activism and advocacy that characterized the period 1975–2000 have been replaced by open hostility; the present moment is fraught with political risk. While the development of information technology opens new possibilities for global networks never before imagined, the women's movement's reach also depends on the perceived relevance of the movement to strategic constituencies. Here differences of class, race and ethnicity have been exacerbated by tensions resulting from the new dichotomies being promoted by a US administration that divides the world into those who are 'with us' and those who are 'against us'. Dichotomies such as good and evil, civilized and uncivilized, Western democracies versus rogue or failed states, place those who are 'against us' at risk of being characterized as terrorists, trying to undermine 'our values'. Effectiveness depends on the politics and praxis of the movement in relation to its relevance and reach. Ultimately, all of this depends on leadership.

In this chapter I shall argue that the relevance and effectiveness of the global women's movement to address the present crisis depend on how it deals with three sets of challenges, which I categorize as substantive, relational and organizational. These challenges emerge from an assessment of the strategies used by the movement over the past twenty years. The issue of leadership will be addressed in the next chapter.

The context: then and now

Then ... The context in which the global women's movement was shaped was one in which the international community came together, within the UN, to address issues that were global in scope, seeking a consensus that would allow states to take joint action on issues of common concern. Within this system the openness to NGOs and civil society organizations was unprecedented, starting with the UN Conference on Environment and Development in 1992. In this context the global women's movement emerged with a politics and praxis that offered new insights and ways of conceptualizing issues derived from an analysis of the diverse experiences of women – the most negatively affected by the issues being addressed. This analysis itself came out of processes of consultation and negotiation between women from diverse backgrounds of race/ethnicity, class, nationality and culture.

Throughout the 1980s, and particularly in the 1990s, while the response of the international community to the emergence of women's movements as political actors was mixed, it was largely open to the insights and analyses offered by these movements. The global women's movement was able to achieve a number of its objectives, particularly in relation to women's role in international development and decision-making, as well as in the area of women's human rights (including issues of violence and reproductive rights). These achievements, however, generated increasing resistance from fundamentalist forces, reinforced at the turn of the century by the capture of the US administration by a strong right-wing Christian coalition.

And now Today the multilateralism and cooperation of the 1990s have been shattered by the emergence of a superpower that acts unilaterally, except when it seeks the cooperation of the international community to underwrite its projects. In one sense, the aggressive militarism of post-9/11 can be read as a clash between patriarchal systems, vying for economic and political supremacy, and willing to use military force to secure it. But given the enormous imbalance of power between the USA and all other countries and regions, it also represents the USA's assertion of political hegemony, parallel to its assertion of economic hegemony through corporate-led globalization.

This clash between extremes of patriarchal power poses problems of human security for everyone. However, women and people of colour in the Third World, as well as in North America and Europe, face particular dangers that intensify the risks to their security.[1] The crisis in reproduction is exacerbated by the crisis in human security, and this is ultimately a crisis in governance, as governments are too weak, too corrupt, or both, to deal effectively with the crises in reproduction and human security in the face of US power.

Another aspect of the post-9/11 world is the threat to civil society organizations. The risk to those who dissent is one part of this. Another, less often discussed, is the vulnerability of CSOs to infiltration and manipulation by those who would recruit well-intentioned people to serve the interests of international capital. This is easily done, and the only protection against it is to be informed, to learn the lessons of history and to have a clear analysis of events on the ground. The latest experience of civil unrest leading to the intervention of US-led military force in Haiti is an example of one of the risks faced by CSOs. I discuss this more fully in the Epilogue.

Origins of the present conjuncture

The origins of the present conjuncture can be traced to trends that emerged in the aftermath of the collapse of the Soviet Union in 1990. Throughout the Cold War, international debates revolved around two axes, the geo-political axis of East–West relations and the political-economic axis of North–South relations. The removal of the East–West axis had two sets of consequences. In economic terms, the collapse of the Soviet economic system removed the socialist alternative to capitalism and strengthened the spread of the neo-liberal macro-economic policy framework that had been launched in the 1980s. At the same time it allowed us to focus attention on North–South relations, not just in geographical terms but also in terms of class. I am speaking here about the relations between rich and poor within as well as between countries. These relations are at the heart of the present debates on neo-liberal, corporate-led globalization.

In the ten years following the collapse of the Soviet economic system, the USA built its economic power through the influence of the US Treasury on the international financial institutions (IFIs) that helped promote the Washington Consensus. The promotion of a common macro-economic policy framework laid the basis for, and facilitated the spread of, neo-liberalism and the restructuring of global economies. The social, economic, political and cultural consequences of this policy framework that were particularly inimical to women's gender interests are described in Chapter 5. The global women's movement was among the first to pay attention to the implications of the change of administration in the USA for women worldwide,[2] and to note the link between economic fundamentalism inherent in global restructuring and the religious fundamentalism which often accompanies it.

Challenges of the present

Substantive challenges In a case study on Chile (Basu 1995), the authors conclude that one of the most important challenges facing the women's movement in the future is:

> The internal articulation and consequent public visibility necessary to enhance and give leverage to women's proposals for social change and (2) the placement of the feminist agenda within a more general framework of social change without any loss of autonomy and specificity and with a modification of the presently gender-specific characteristics of power relations.

In many countries, organizing around a feminist agenda has, for want of a coherent analysis, lacked clarity. On the other hand, some of the most successful advocacy has been the result of analyses that clarify the links between economic, socio-cultural and political factors.

The current challenge for women's advocates is to pay attention to the politics of redistribution no less than to the politics of recognition. Because of the tendency of Western feminists to emphasize issues of recognition, those of distributive justice have tended to be overlooked. On the other hand, feminist researchers from developing countries *have* addressed these issues, including in their work not only an analysis of the colonial and neo-colonial relations that are implicated in the subordination of the largest proportion of women in these countries, but an analysis of the macro-economic policy framework as well.

Nevertheless, much more needs to be done to show the linkages between gender relations and the economic, social, cultural and political systems and structures that serve to perpetuate and escalate crises in reproduction and human security.

Specifically, in the present conjuncture, there is particular need to articulate the linkages between gender relations, women's subordination, racism and the problems of poverty, the low priority given to social services in the public sector, violence and militarism. The substantive work will have to focus on a number of themes, including:

- Finding a model of human security that does not strip us of our human rights. The global women's movement has to help those who seek peace and justice to understand that these cannot be achieved without addressing issues of racism and class, and the sexism that is integral to both.
- In terms of racism and sexism, we have to show how, underlying the use of overwhelming military force to counter terrorism and sadistic dictatorships, as well as acts of individual and state terrorism in Iraq and Israel, is a violence that is both patriarchal and racist.
- In terms of class and sexism, we have to show how the

exploitation of women's time, labour and sexuality underpins capitalist exploitation.

This calls for important and critical work to be done by feminists in the academy in two areas in particular, racism and sexism, and for the integration of this work into a variety of fields. Stuart Hall's description of how feminism (as well as work on race) transformed cultural studies shows increasing recognition of what feminism has to offer to a wide range of disciplinary fields. What is needed, in addition to these academic pursuits, is a more conscious linking of such work with the political work of women's movements.

Recently a strong argument has been advanced for the adoption of an approach to women that links feminist studies, cultural studies and Third World/development studies.[3] The combination of the three draws on the strengths of each, and fills gaps that occur when they are treated separately:

- the contribution of feminist studies to the enrichment of scholarship in a number of fields – not just the humanities and social sciences;[4]
- the attention paid by cultural studies to the importance of analysing cultures within their contexts and focusing on the perspectives of people derived from lived experience;
- the use of 'insights of social sciences and historical schools such as dependency and world system theory and modes of production analysis to argue that global and international processes need to be seen *in situ*, with a focus on the countries of the South'.[5]

Specifically, a 'Women, Culture and Development' (WCD) approach would help resolve some of the dilemmas within women's movements by addressing in a more useful way

- issues of class, race/ethnicity and nationality;
- the links between production and reproduction;
- issues of power, conflict and the larger social, cultural and political contexts of women's lives;

- the centrality of family, community and religion in women's lives;
- women's agency 'that may not just perpetuate inequalities but also challenge them'.[6]

For example, Kum-Kum Bhavnani argues that 'In integrating production with reproduction alongside women's agency, a WCD approach can interrogate issues of ethnicity, gender, religion, sexuality and livelihood simultaneously, thereby providing a nuanced examination of social processes ... that may provide clearer ideas for a transformative development that attends to aspects of people's lives beyond the economic.'[7]

Relational The global women's movement is one part of a larger multinational movement that cuts across race and ethnicity, class, gender and generation in common opposition to the hegemonic spread of global capitalism. In part, its ability to contribute is determined by its ability to appeal to others in that movement. However, women's movements have a basic problem in relation to other social movements – the fundamental position of women's movements is for justice for women (or opposition to the asymmetry of gender relations within patriarchal society). This challenge to male privilege is inevitably uncomfortable and even alienating – to many women as well as to men.

If its purpose is to help the larger movement to understand the centrality of gender justice to the broad project of global justice, the global women's movement will have to resolve the tensions between those within women's movements who focus on identity politics and those who use feminist politics to articulate and advance the larger social project for social justice,[8] from the perspective of poor women living in the economic South. In relation to the movement for global justice at this conjuncture, a global women's movement – whatever the situation at local levels – must show that its goal is not to build the women's movement per se but to contribute to strengthening the movement for global justice; it can do this by offering its insights and analyses of the ways in which the exploitation of women's time, labour and sexuality serves the purposes of corporate greed, political repression and a culture of violence.

While feminist politics must be worked out within women's movements, it is the widest dispersion of this politics that the global women's movement seeks. This is not an easy task, but it will be less difficult if feminists are careful that our strategies and tactics are not unnecessarily alienating to women in our movement as well as to the larger movement.

The following relationships are crucial if the feminist-led global women's movement is to contribute to strengthening the larger movement for global justice:

- with women within and outside women's movements;
- with young women;
- with mainstream NGOs and social movements;
- with the state;
- with multinational institutions.

RELATIONSHIPS BETWEEN FEMINISTS AND WOMEN WITHIN AND OUTSIDE WOMEN'S MOVEMENTS In my definition of women's movements (Chapter 2) I excluded women's organizations that work against the goals of gender equality and equity but included all women who seek to improve the conditions and position of women. Many of these women are uncomfortable with feminism and with feminist politics. The truth is that the word 'feminism' is problematic, particularly in some countries of the economic South. It has negative connotations in terms of class, race and nationality; it implies being anti-male and anti-family. That these images are media distortions, intended to discourage feminist organizing, has not changed popular opinion about feminism. Nevertheless, many women, while distancing themselves from the word, use feminist analysis and strategies in their work. As bell hooks puts it, 'We can live and act in feminist resistance without ever using the word "feminism".'[9]

In short, there is a tension between feminists and other women within women's movements who are more ambivalent about challenging prevailing gender relations, and certainly about some of the feminist language concerning these relations. Some feminists are also insensitive to differences of class, race, ethnicity and nationality, and alienate women with whom they share goals of social justice. Nevertheless we have to acknowledge that feminist politics has been the driving force in women's organizing, often infusing more traditional women's groups and even NGOs and other social movements with clarity about the systemic links between various kinds of oppression. The movement will be weakened unless this is acknowledged (even implicitly) by those who are fearful of being labelled 'feminist'.

A challenge for feminist leadership within women's movements in general, and the global women's movement in particular, will therefore be to demystify feminism by confronting media misrepresentations, showing how they are used not only to divide women but also to discredit a movement that has been strengthened by feminist politics.

Another major challenge for women's movements is diversity and difference among women. As I have argued, the processes that led to the evolution of an international, trans-national and global women's movement have been of on-going conflict, confrontation and negotiation between groups of women claiming their own identities. However, much more needs to be done, especially in relation to class and race/ethnicity.

In the present context there is need for a special focus on those women most affected – poor women, women of colour living in the North as well as those living in the South, and women living under Muslim laws. The capacity of the global women's movement to be relevant and to contribute to solutions to the present crises will be determined by the extent to which women from these groups exercise leadership within the movement. Special attention will therefore have to be paid to the involvement of women from groups that have so far tended to be marginalized within the movement. I am thinking particularly of women from indigenous and peasant women's movements, from labour unions and from religious communities that challenge oppressive relationships within these communities and sectors. The fact is that there are well-established networks in all these communities and sectors;

the challenge facing the global women's movement is to ensure that they are all well represented and have a stronger voice within the movement. Their help in incorporating their experience into the analysis is also vital. The goal must be what Angela Miles has termed 'integrative or transformative feminisms':

> feminisms committed to specifically feminist, women-associated values as well as to equality. Since they propose these values as alternatives to the dominant ones, they can challenge not just women's exclusion from social structures and rewards but the very nature of these structures and rewards. Theirs are ... politics that go beyond pressure for a single group and address the whole of society.[10]

In order to be more inclusive, the global women's movement must pay more attention to language and location and North–South divides.

Language. The English language has taken on hegemonic power, and this excludes a majority of the women of the world. The problem with language is also that many words have a patriarchal meaning, and it is often difficult to find words to describe women's experiences. Moreover, many of the words and concepts put forward by feminists have been co-opted and made to mean something entirely different. 'Empowerment' is one of these; 'gender' is another.

Location. In many countries, race and class divide the women who operate within bureaucratic centres of patriarchal power from those outside. Yet these institutions often contain feminists challenging patriarchal power from within. Strategic links can yield good results, since carefully thought-through 'insider-outsider' strategies are essential for political restructuring and social transformation.

North–South divides. Although the differences between North and South have to be modified in light of the widening gap between rich and poor in countries of the North as well as in the South, the legacy of colonial relations between 'centre' and 'periphery' nations remains. Indeed, neo-liberal globalization has created a new class structure in international relations, one between the beneficiaries of globalization and those left out.[11] As I have stated above, all of this is sharpened in the context of the emergence of US 'imperialism' and the push for stronger bonds between 'Western democracies' to counter 'terrorism'.

RELATIONSHIPS WITH YOUNG WOMEN One of the most impressive features of the movement for global justice is the overwhelming presence of young people, many of them young women. At the same time, an ongoing concern within women's movements is how to attract more young women to the movement. While many young women in leadership positions within youth movements view women's movements as irrelevant or alienating, young women are increasingly visible in the global women's movement and their leadership brings new energy and creativity.

There are major issues of inclusion and exclusion between young and older women. This generation gap is often related to personal histories: those who took on leadership roles in the past twenty years have developed close bonds of solidarity out of their shared struggles during the Decade for Women and the UN conferences of the 1990s. Younger women feel excluded. At the same time, young women may see the world differently, and certainly face issues that are outside the experience of their mothers. Many, having benefited from the earlier struggles for women's liberation and gender equality, take these freedoms and opportunities for granted. Their relationships with men, personally and in the workplace, may not be as demeaning as those experienced by earlier generations of women. Many, ignorant of the shifts in women's movements to broader agendas, feel that other issues, such as the environment, HIV-AIDS or globalization, are more important. For these young women there is little or no understanding of how the structure of women's exclusion/ exploitation/subordination is an inherent part of the economic and political structures that contribute to the issues that concern them. They certainly do not experience themselves as excluded, oppressed or subordinated. Only personal experience can shift this overweening confidence (and it does).

One of the problems in relation to young women and the

women's movement is the tendency to see the issue as one of 'incorporating' young women into the women's movement, and to overlook the fact that young women have their own networks. A more appropriate approach might be to acknowledge that the participation of young women in women's movements need not be limited to their incorporation into women's organizations, and to encourage the participation of young women's organizations in the projects of the larger women's movement and vice versa – for women's organizations to participate in projects initiated by young women.

A challenge to the global women's movement is how to bridge the gap with young women in the larger movement for global justice in ways that empower younger women, without negating the valuable experience of the past twenty years, which has brought us this far. This is especially important since, as a social movement with the potential for transformational politics, the women's movement has only just begun to understand the systemic linkages that need to be challenged, which means that there is need to build on work already done. While it is true that each generation must work on its own agendas, much valuable time and energy are lost in processes of reinvention. Maybe the global women's movement needs to listen more closely to what young women are saying, and be prepared to respond to their questions rather than offer solutions.[12]

With young women featuring as the chief victims of the HIV-AIDS pandemic, the involvement of young women in the global women's movement is crucial if the movement is to give leadership in this area. On-going work will rest with the coming generation.

RELATIONSHIPS WITH MAINSTREAM NGOS AND SOCIAL MOVEMENTS We cannot build a movement for social transformation without making strategic alliances with men. In any event, in the present conjuncture our relationship with men in the movement for global justice is crucial. A starting point may be to distinguish between men in the social movement who are open to partnership with feminist leadership and those who are not, and to make strategic alliances with those who understand that there is no justice for anyone if there is no justice for women.

There are many men who understand that patriarchy wounds and dehumanizes men as much as it does women, and that there is a continuum between sexism and violence. These men also understand that policies that place the interests of corporations before those of people affect women in specific ways, and are open to accepting women's leadership in the definition of issues and strategies.

An increasing number of men are recognizing the ways in which patriarchy limits our understanding of human possibilities, and the contribution of feminism to projects that seek social justice and a better life for all. Amartya Sen's work on women's agency is important, as is Michael Kaufman's on masculinity. Kaufman sees the link between women's agency and 'the shifting of social and economic priorities to the long-term needs of our children, the nurturing of communities, stewardship of our environment, and an end to the proliferation of weapons, massively destructive or not'.[13] He also argues for new models of manhood if we are to address the issue of violence.

In his work on revolutions, John Foran recognizes that one of the reasons they fall short of the dream of social justice is 'differences among revolutionaries about how to construct a better society – that is, their inevitable flaws as people, and their *enmeshment in structures of patriarchy and racism*'[14] (emphasis mine).

Unfortunately, the men who are willing to identify publicly with a feminist agenda are few and unevenly distributed. A global women's movement has a special role to play in identifying and affirming these allies and helping extend their work to other countries and regions where it is needed. A major challenge to a global women's movement is to work with these men to strengthen their analysis, and to help in the creation of a network of men who understand that the struggle for women's agency is intrinsic to all struggles for social transformation.

RELATIONSHIP WITH THE STATE There has always been tension between those feminists who are deeply suspicious of the state and other patriarchal institutions they rightly perceive as patriarchal, such as the church, the family and the legal system. For these feminists, activism is, by definition, oppositional. On the other hand, for feminists who focus on specific goals such as women's suffrage, access to education, credit and employment, reproductive health and ending discrimination, activism has included critical but constructive engagement with patriarchal institutions, with a view to their reform. However, the divide between reform and revolution is too simplistic for a process as complex as challenging gender-based asymmetries and hierarchies.

Critics of feminist engagement with mainstream institutions and policy-making processes argue that such interaction at best takes the edge off feminist politics and at worst leads to co-optation.[15] In her reflection on the five-year review of the Fourth World Conference of Women held in New York in June 2000, Nighat Said Khan focused on the contradictions and de-politicization of a movement that was supposedly about challenging patriarchy:

> The question is whether we have this critique any longer – of patriarchy, the state or the UN – or whether we are only interested in being included in the system.[16]

From Latin America, Virginia Vargas has drawn attention to the ambivalence of the state in relation to women and gender issues: on the one hand the state is a powerful instrument of equality through its laws, policies and actors; on the other hand it is a machine that reproduces inequality through its norms and the traditional gender practices reflected in its actions:

> For feminist movements, the relationship with the political-public sphere, particularly the State, has been one of the most complex and stressing issues. At a certain level, it has generated great polar-isation, producing the first great internal 'rupture'. However, at another level, it has managed to place several feminist proposals in the political-public sphere. That is why opinions are varied, oppos-ing, and sometimes ambivalent, regarding the importance of what is attained, and the fear of what is lost.[17]

One aspect of the link between the state and the goals of women's movement has indeed been the bureaucratization of the movement, the trend towards institutionalization and professionalization in the women's movement, the risks to the autonomy of the movement, and the challenge of keeping alive

> the transforming radical nature of feminist thought and action as we simultaneously penetrate into political spaces and, as politicians, negotiate and reach agreements with the existing powers, with real democracies, with agendas that movements present.[18]

Using her experience in the Asian region in the process leading up to the 1995 conference in Beijing, Nighat Khan explores how 'working within the system changes not only our positions but our strategies'.[19] At the same time, if feminist politics has the objective of challenging and changing gender power relations, and seeing this reflected in public policy, there is no avoiding engagement in mainstream processes. The point at issue is to recognize that change does not occur without the political pressure that can be exerted only from outside the mainstream ('History is made by people and people's movements ... confronting the status quo',[20] while acknowledging the value of having allies within mainstream institutions. Indeed a progressive government *can* make revolutionary changes in gender relations.

The strategy of working from within as well as from the outside is one of the possibilities offered by a movement that transcends the normal boundaries of class, race, nationality, and institutional location. A movement that includes a rich diversity of individuals that may not have institutional affiliations has the flexibility required for a complex strategy which draws on both the access of key individuals to the seats and centres of patriarchal power and the radicalism of those who would neither seek nor receive such access.

There is also no gainsaying the fact that women need the state. This is especially true for women in the South.[21] The dilemma for women's movements in the South in relation to the state is that on the one hand, the majority of women lack resources and therefore must depend on the state to provide the basic services essential to women's multiple roles; on the other hand, women must be careful that this dependence is not used to reinforce traditional roles within the family.

This is a particular challenge when women's movements are part of the 'struggle within the struggle', women's struggles within larger struggles. Again and again we read of the active participation of women within the larger struggles for independence, democracy, social justice and against racism, only to learn later of their exclusion from the benefits of those struggles. In fact in some instances, as in the case of the transition from socialism to capitalism in the countries of the former Soviet bloc, there have been reversals in the rights women gained under socialism, especially in the area of reproductive rights, since pro-family/ natalist agendas have become part of 'nation-building'. As Elzbieta Matynia points out, a 'by-product' of the rise of nationalist ideologies is that the rights of the nation as a community are given priority over those of the citizen. 'Women are defined here as bearers of the community's distinctive ethnic lineage and are therefore considered a vital factor in national survival.'[22]

According to Matynia, nationalism underlies the anti-abortion policies introduced in the post-communist period, as well as the systematic rape of Muslim women in Bosnia as an instrument of ethnic cleansing.

But while women's movements must be wary of state power, the fact of the matter is that women's vision of a model of development that is equitable, participatory and sustainable clearly depends on state actors for realization, and it has been women's historic role to keep issues of equity and distribution on the development agenda.[23]

In the past, and in the context of the global conferences of the 1990s and beyond, the global women's movement's engagement with the state has been a necessary focus for its work. In its platform for the 1995 conference, DAWN called for 'reform of the state' as one part of a three-tiered strategy directed to 'states, markets and civil society'. UN conventions, resolutions, programmes and plans of action have given women important tools for advancing their struggles. The human rights framework is particularly helpful in some countries. It also has the advantage of providing a universal standard against which a country's performance might be judged.

In the present conjuncture, and in the context of states that seem too weak to stand up to the domination of the superpower, feminist activists who have been critical of the state may have to rethink the relationship between the movement and the state. Whatever the pros and cons of engagement between women's movement and state, the world public opinion that expressed itself so strongly in the anti-war movement cannot be truly effective without the support of powerful states. The fact that even the opposition of the members of the Security Council failed to stop the USA invading Iraq should not detract from the fact that this opposition did succeed in denying international legitimacy for the war. In the present conjuncture and in the context of multilateral institutions like the IMF and the WTO, it is only state power that can protect civil society from the abuses of a superpower acting like a rogue state, or from exploitation by trans-national corporations.

RELATIONSHIPS WITH MULTINATIONAL INSTITUTIONS Engagement with multinational institutions is imperative for a global women's movement. Local movements depend on having their issues raised at this level. The challenge for the global movement is to ensure its links to local levels, to ensure that the global is part of the local and vice versa: a movement back and forth between these two arenas is essential if the global is not to become something separate from local movements. In relation to the UN, there is the on-going work of monitoring agreements and proposals won in the international conferences of the 1990s, while in relation to the IFIs and the WTO the global women's movement must continue to challenge the ways in which their policies and programmes contradict their statements about equity and global justice.

Organizational issues
POPULAR EDUCATION AND ORGANIZING AT THE LOCAL LEVEL Today's global issues require global advocacy and action. We also

know that without strong local and regional women's movements, work at a global level is futile. The global women's movement is well aware of the importance of building the links between local and global. What need to be emphasized, however, are the participatory methodologies that can engage grassroots women in more meaningful dialogue and debate about larger structures and systems and allow their concerns to inform global advocacy. There have been some good examples of this kind of mobilization in campaigns against domestic violence and the global campaign for women's rights.

In the present conjuncture, grassroots movements become points of resistance to the hegemonic tendencies of neo-liberalism and globalization. In many countries it is in out of the way places, at local levels, that women are most creative in finding ways to exercise the greatest autonomy. As local communities seek to grapple with globalization in its broadest form, a 'politics of place' has emerged as women work to defend themselves, their families and communities.[24] These experiences are rich in the insights and inspiration they might offer a global women's movement. A major challenge for a global women's movement that seeks to extend its reach is therefore to find a methodology that creates and strengthens the links between organizing and advocacy at local and global levels, without interfering with context-specific survival strategies and visions of betterment.

For women involved in the global women's movement it is also essential that they return to their own 'roots' from time to time, for reflection, renewal and reconnection with realities on the ground. Reflection is an important part of any process of learning. It is an activity that must be undertaken by women both as individuals and as members of a small collective: as an individual activity it is part of the process of personal transformation; undertaken together with a small group of trusted friends and colleagues, it is part of the process of consciousness-raising/conscientization that links the personal to the political and strengthens women's agency *vis-à-vis* the linked structures that subordinate and marginalize women.

COALITION POLITICS The formation of issue-based networks has produced some of the most effective organizing, linking work at local level to global organizing. Nevertheless much more needs to be done to link women across the divides of class, race and ethnicity, and ideology, as well as linking the issue-based networks.

Identity comes before solidarity. And as suggested above, more efforts must be made by the leadership of a global women's movement to ensure that the movement is more representative of the diversity that exists within it. In the present context this means ensuring more prominent leadership roles for the women most negatively affected by the forces that are currently in ascendance.

FINANCIAL RESOURCES Another problem has been the lack of a financial base to ensure the sustainability of a global women's movement. While local movements can flourish without financial resources, a global movement cannot. Travel and communications are obviously costly. The UN Decade for Women provided the resources for many activities, including research, projects, meetings and travel. It is difficult to imagine how these activities, and the events that served to focus activities, could have happened without these resources. The linking of women across national boundaries was probably the single most important element in the emerging global women's movement.

At the same time, there are a number of challenges inherent in the financing of a global women's movement. One is how to avoid competition for funds between local and global initiatives. Organizing at both levels is equally important and can, at best, be complementary. Another problem is how to avoid dependence on external funding, especially in the case of Third World women's organizing, when these resources come from Northern institutions and governments. Virginia Vargas has drawn attention to the ways in which the 'NGOization' and dependence on external funding of the feminist movement in Latin America can blunt the political edge of the movement. Another aspect of this, especially in the present context, is how to ensure that funding is not used by the rich and powerful to build civil society organizations that serve their political and financial purposes. Clearly, some sources will be taboo for feminist organizing.

The present context is one in which financial resources are particularly limited, especially if the global women's movement is questioning the value of another UN conference on women. A major challenge for the movement will therefore be how to find sources of finance that are supportive of feminist organizing at a global level. The emergence of women's funds provides a partial solution, but this problem will inevitably persist.

INFORMATION AND COMMUNICATIONS TECHNOLOGIES (ICTS) It is obvious that the new information and communications technologies have made global networking and organizing possible. Advances in these technologies have transformed the work of global networks within the global women's movement. While unevenness of access to the Internet is inevitable, given the unevenness in the distribution of incomes and technology worldwide, the global women's movement has been among those fortunate enough to be able to make full use of this technology from its earliest stages.

In the present context, when mainstream media are heavily censored and controlled to promote a particular kind of propaganda, ICTs have been invaluable as an alternative source of information: activists know, for instance, that protests against the war were continuing even as the US-led coalition claimed victory; and we could get another version of events in places like Venezuela and Haiti, Afghanistan and Iraq. ICTs have the potential to be one of the most effective tools for a global women's movement seeking to communicate that the negative forces that jeopardize the lives of millions of people around the world have their roots in sexism.

Paradoxes and dilemmas

A number of dilemmas and paradoxes remain within women's movements, including the global women's movement. Major sources of tension within the movements are:

* institutionalization versus autonomy;

- equality versus difference;
- universal and specific contents of citizenship;
- negotiating local–global spaces;
- women and the family.

They are not easily resolved; and many would question whether it is even necessary to seek their resolution. After all, in a diverse and complex world, acceptance of paradoxes and dilemmas, contradictions and complexity, is what saves us from dogmatism and intolerance.

This is not the place to discuss issues as complex as these. However, there is one set of issues on which a global women's

---

Women, family and motherhood: a reflection

Feminists have been accused of being 'anti-family', and this is an accusation that must be honestly addressed if feminist leadership is to be relevant in broader women's movements and women's lives. The majority of women are comfortable with traditional roles within the family; certainly they value family relationships, require stability for raising their children and security in their old age, all of which can be experienced within loving, caring families. But family relationships can also be abusive, limiting women's options and even placing their lives and those of their children in jeopardy.

Can women combine strong commitment to their families with asserting their specific needs as women? The answer depends on a number of factors, including the degree of patriarchal control within the family, whether women have children, or, more broadly, where women are in their life cycle.

The degree of patriarchal control within the family Class, culture, economics and the political system mediate patriarchy, and the degree of patriarchal control within the family varies with these factors. The subject is full of paradox. Writing about the situation of women in Poland, Hungary and Czechoslovakia under communism, Elzbieta Matynia notes that the church and the family often represented 'spheres of freedom' for women, although they have now become 'spheres of constraint'.[25]

Under colonialism, missionaries promoted women's submission and subordination to male authority, but they also provided education for girls, an important precondition for their emancipation. Industrialization is often exploitative of women's labour, but it also creates opportunities for women's liberation from oppressive family structures.

In Western European societies, women's liberation has had to take the form of resistance to domestication and subordination within the patriarchal family. However, in most other cultures and countries, women have not been so confined, nor has patriarchy been experienced quite as oppressively as it is in societies where economic and political power are centred in the hands of an elite. This is exacerbated when that elite has also been able to impose their rule on others through colonialism.

In colonized societies stratified by class, race and ethnicity, therefore, women cannot easily separate their struggles as women from the larger struggles, against other oppressive forces. Indeed, many women's movements had their origins within these struggles, where women both learned about oppression and developed the skills to resist it.

In situations in which whole groups and categories of people are oppressed by class, race and ethnicity, women's solidarity with men has sometimes precluded consciousness of their own oppression. In any event, in these situations the forces that oppress women include class, colonialism and racism, and these forces have to be engaged, along with sexism. This is why women of colour and Third World women often have a better understanding of the complexity of oppressive systems, and consequently resist the exclusive focus on sexism.

Motherhood and women's values A major tension in women's movements is between those women who are mobilized 'on the basis of motherhood and the political virtue of women's values'[26] and those who are concerned about the price women have always paid for this kind of 'essentializing'. In all societies, women's reality includes involvement in the care and nurturing of children, partly because of the biological imperative, but also because of gender ideology within patriarchal society. At the same time, the association between women and motherhood has been used to justify the domestication and subordination of women: the gender division of labour that restricts women to the home, the denial of women's full human rights (including reproductive rights and economic rights), compulsory heterosexism, the use of pro-natalist policies to coerce women to have more children than they might want, and much more. However, the fact that this involvement with children and family has been used against women's agency does not negate their attachment to children and family, nor the values associated with family relationships.

The care of children gives importance to a set of values that have come to be mostly associated with women: safety, security, concern for others, compassion, cooperation. This also determines a set of priorities that are again associated with women: food and water, housing, health and education – the basic requirements for reproducing the human species. These are basic human needs, but women, because of their assigned responsibility for caring for children, are the ones with the most at stake when these needs are not met. Women are therefore most likely to offer the strongest defence for their primacy over the allocation of resources to armaments and other items that carry status value. Nevertheless, one might still feel uncomfortable speaking of 'women's values' as if all women share similar values, or as if men do not share some of the values that are normally associated with women: caring, compassion, cooperation.

Women's life-cycle Often the tensions between women in relation to the family are intergenerational, and connected to where women are in their life-cycle. We need to consider the realities of women's life-cycle in judging and negotiating the risks and tensions inherent in strategies such as challenging patriarchy, promoting sexual and reproductive rights, and engagement with the state, to name a few. Certainly, women with children (especially young children) often have different priorities from those without, or from older women, especially if they are poor.

These issues are crucial in movement building and in determining the appropriateness of various strategies and tactics at particular moments in time and in particular spaces and places. A life-cycle approach might lead to greater sensitivity and lessen tensions between different groups of women.

Resolution The threefold crisis we face today – in reproduction, human security and governance – is closely linked to women's reality in relation to their families. We have to construct a feminist politics based on this reality. The articulation of the values associated with women's reality comes from that process – and must be seen to originate in feminist politics, rather than from patriarchal institutions.

By not taking up these issues in the past, feminists have left the field open to patriarchal institutions like the church and the state. These institutions have exploited women's time, labour and sexuality in their own interests – they look to women to produce and reproduce the 'manpower' required for their congregations, factories, armies or nations. It is time for women to recapture this ground, so that the objectification of children, and their own subordination, can be ended.

We have to find a way of affirming both motherhood and those values associated with women without essentializing women or playing into the hands of those who would define women in terms of their wombs! The global women's movement has to find a way to bridge the potential gap between women who want to affirm the values of caring, compassion and cooperation, and those who give priority to struggling against the patriarchal institutions that oppress women. I believe this must involve:

- clarifying the values traditionally associated with women;
- articulating them as part of a process of feminist politics; and
- reclaiming them as our own, so that they are not delivered to us by patriarchal institutions.

Certainly, women's movements must be careful not to concede concerns about the family to right-wing ideologues. We might start by challenging and replacing the myth of the 'good' woman with the vision of the 'free' woman.[27]

movement (see p. 161) must seek clarity and perhaps resolution: those related to the family and motherhood.

Conclusion

The global women's movement is, by definition, more limited in its relevance, reach and effectiveness in certain ways than are local women's movements. At the same time, there are things that only a global women's movement can attempt, and ways in which it can be supportive of and strengthen local movements. It must acknowledge these limitations and strengths even as it confronts the changing context in which it operates. The present conjuncture calls for the movement to rethink its strategies in terms of substance, relationships and organization if it is to continue to be relevant and effective in a world that needs its leadership as never before.

There are nevertheless challenges not easily addressed, and dilemmas not easily resolved, reflecting the complexities and contradictions of a movement that must engage in continuous struggle if it is to represent the lived experience of its constituency.

Notes

1 Seldom recognized are the risks to Muslim women from extremist factions within Islam, who use Western injustice as an excuse for the reinforcing of patriarchal control on 'their women', the protectors of the 'culture'.

2 At the World Social Forum in 2000, which coincided with the inauguration of the new US President, the women's movement staged a major demonstration against one of his first acts, the reintroduction of the 'gag' rule, which would stop US aid to any family planning programme offering abortion.

3 Bhavnani et al. (2003).

4 This includes the natural sciences as well as many professional schools such as medicine, psychiatry, psychology, education and law.

5 Bhavnani et al. (2003), p. 7.

6 Ibid., p. 5.

7 Ibid., p. 8.

8 At the DAWN's inaugural Training Institute (2003), some young women made the distinction between 'women's rights advocates' (WRA) and 'feminists'; they viewed feminists as being concerned with what Gita Sen describes as the broader social project, and WRA as more focused on identity politics.

9 hooks (1994), p. 62.

10 Miles (1996), p. xi.

11 Reference is often made to winners and losers in the processes of globalization.

12 Participation in DAWN's inaugural Training Institute in Feminist Advocacy left me greatly impressed, and encouraged by the possibility for respectful relations across generations.

13 Michael Kaufman, 'Manhood and War',<www.michael kaufman.com>.

14 Foran, quoted in Bhavnani et al. (2003), p. 269.

15 Zed Book's recent publication (2002) on women's movements and international relations, *Common Ground or Mutual Exclusion?*, Braig and Wolte (eds), includes a number of excellent articles on these debates. See especially the chapter by Nighat Said Khan, pp. 35–45.

16 Ibid., p. 37.

17 Vargas (2000; see DAWN website), pp. 41–2.

18 Ibid., p. 55.

19 Khan, in Braig and Wolte (2002), p. 38.

20 Ibid., p. 37.

21 It is possible that those Third World women who have come out of the anti-colonial struggles of the 1950s–1960s have a different experience of the state. This may be particularly true in countries, such as those of the English-speaking Caribbean, where the first political parties evolved from the labour movement.

22 Matynia, in Basu (1995), p. 381.

23 It has been noted that issues of equity and redistribution, subjects that had virtually vanished from the economic literature for the past two decades were once again central to the discussions on 'financing for development' in the lead-up to the UN conference held in Monterrey, Mexico, in 2002. However, women have never stopped raising these issues as integral to their agendas and development proposals.

24 Society for International Development (2001).

25 Matynia, in Basu (1995), pp. 374–404.

26 DAWN Informs Supplement for WSF 2002.

27 Nan Peacocke's poem, written to mark IWD 1985, makes this distinction; see p. 191 below.

9 | Leadership for moving forward

The question to be considered here is: How might a global women's movement strengthen and renew itself in order to make a contribution to solving the problems of the present conjuncture? Previously, I have outlined the challenges to be addressed. Here I want to focus on issues of leadership. No matter how good the strategies, the challenges cannot be met without leadership. What kind of leadership? Where might it be found? How might it be strengthened and renewed? What is the special role of leadership at the global level, as distinct from leadership within local and regional movements?

What kind of leadership?

Many call for women's leadership, but we all have experience of women in leadership positions who act no differently from their male colleagues. Indeed, many women in formal positions of leadership are constrained in their ability to act in the interests of the majority of people, and specifically in the interest of women. Most of the women in political leadership owe their position to their conformity with male models of leadership and their acceptance of the status quo. They can be trusted to play the game according to the rules; trusted not to rock the boat.

We also need a concept of leadership that goes beyond the formal definitions of leadership to include women at every level, and one that understands leadership as *facilitating* rather than *directing*.

Over the past few years I have been reflecting on the kind of women's leadership needed for social transformation towards a world where:

money does not define value nor legislate survival ... where all

In 1974, when I was appointed by the Government of Jamaica as an Advisor on women's affairs, I had never heard the word 'feminism'. But the bureaucrats who thought it 'safe' to appoint to this post someone with no identification with the women's movement never reckoned on the transforming power of feminism. It was to change my life as well as my understanding of the world. I learned more about the workings of the political economy of post-colonialism and about social relations from my work on women's issues than I did from university courses in political economics and social work. But most of all feminism gave me a politics that transformed a shy, fairly conventional, professional woman into an activist for social justice.

the categories and processes of parasitism and hate – racism, classism, ageism, ablism, xenophobia, homophobia – are regarded as belonging to a shameful past ... where war is recognized as expressing unnecessary patriarchal syndromes of dominance and submission in a ridiculously sexualized death ritual using phallic technological instruments, guns and missiles of ever greater proportions ... where the psychosis of patriarchy is recognized, healed, and no longer validated as the norm.[1]

While this vision of a world free of exploitation, intolerance and violence articulates values that appear to be humanistic rather than exclusively related to women, they are feminist in their association of these values as counter to patriarchy. In short, they relate the roots of exploitation, intolerance and violence to patriarchy and its construction of 'woman' as 'other'. This prototype of 'otherness' is also applied to those of races, ethnicities, cultures and classes that differ from the model of those in control – males that are white, Christian and from the ruling class.

I therefore define the type of women's leadership for social transformation as feminist leadership. My definition is as follows:

'transformational leadership' is feminist leadership with a passion for justice, a commitment to change things, beginning with oneself. Each part is important.

Why *feminist*? Transformation is a neutral term. It is meaningless unless we say what it is we want to transform. To do this we need an analysis. For the purposes of challenging patriarchy it must be feminist analysis – an analysis of male power that links this to other forms of oppression.

Why a *passion for justice*? Leadership must feel passionately about social justice, and must see that there can be no social justice without justice for women.

Why a *commitment to change things*? Because many people feel passionately about social justice without being driven to take action; the definition must include a commitment to act for change.

Why a commitment to *personal change*? Because personal transformation must be the beginning of social transformation; because working for social justice is full of risk, and we can only do this work if we find a source of power within ourselves that does not depend on the approval of others, that cannot be taken away by external forces.

Feminist leadership

A great deal has been written about difference and diversity between women and between and within their movements. However, one thing unites all elements, and that is a common opposition to women's subordination, a common vision. Feminism is a historical process, manifest in many different and varied agendas depending on the circumstances in which women's struggles arise. These many feminisms embody differing understandings as to the source of women's oppression. What I want to draw attention to here is the arrival of a global feminist politics that addresses the present conjuncture of forces. This is the first time in history that a crisis so clearly related to women's struggles for economic justice, and democracy linked to gender justice, has appeared. Feminist leadership has brought us to an understanding of these relationships, and to addressing the larger social project for transformation. The task for feminist leadership now is to articulate a more consistent assertion of the role of women's agency in challenging the hegemonic relationships underlying the present crisis. I define this as the feminist politics of the global women's movement.

Feminist politics derives from feminist analysis, which starts with an analysis of patriarchy. Although patriarchy is mediated by race, class and culture,[2] it is nevertheless a system that privileges the practices, attributes and values associated with patriarchal concepts of masculinity while devaluing those normally associated with women's social role – caring, compassion, cooperation, gentleness.

Patriarchy, reflected through all the structures and institutions of our world, is a system that glorifies domination, control, violence, competitiveness and greed. It dehumanizes men as much as it denies women their agency. It is the system that has made the world the dangerous place it is today, a world where fear and violence too often obliterate trust and nurturance. In a world ruled by greed, fear, intolerance and force, changes of regime represent changes of degrees of jeopardy to people's safety and well-being. What has happened in the USA since 9/11 shows how easily democracy itself can be subverted by the manipulation of fear.

Feminist analysis recognizes the role of ideology in the construction of definitions of the male and female, and how the ideology of patriarchy is dispersed and reproduced through a gender ideology that lies at the centre of human socialization, providing the framework for hierarchy, authoritarianism and dichotomies. In the public domain, gender ideology is continuously produced, reproduced and reinforced through institutions such as the family,[3] the school, the market, the state, the judiciary, religious institutions and the media, but the starting point in the process of socialization is the household. Here a network of customs and traditions, cultural practices, laws and institutions constructs the female as subordinate to the male and ascribes to her responsibility for the reproduction of her own subordination and for asymmetrical relations between men and women. The woman lays down the foundations of patriarchal control in the private domain through her earliest interactions with her male partner and children.

Gender ideology makes women the carriers of the culture of male superiority and privilege, and women – through their acceptance of this ideology, which makes them believe they need men as lovers and fathers of their children, as providers and protectors – are heavily invested in this. Women hesitate to act on their own behalf because they do not easily jeopardize the safety, security and well-being of their children or their families. The church and other institutions of society reinforce this through the ideology of the 'good mother'.

The exploitation of women's time, labour and sexuality is fundamental to the continuation of the dominant political economy.

- Because women are socialized to do domestic work and take care of people, the state can transfer responsibility for family health and nutrition to the household, where the labour does not have to be paid.
- The market capitalizes on poor women's desperate need for income, and the notion of the 'male bread-winner', to pay women the lowest wages and treat them as a reserve labour force.
- State, market and civil society combine to manipulate women's sexuality – their relations with men, children and other women, their image of themselves – in the service of the dominant ideology.

In the past few years feminist scholarship has begun to explore and reveal these links between women's subordination and the forces that perpetuate the exclusion and subordination of whole sectors of society (even whole countries and continents). Feminist analysis therefore suggests that there can be no social transformation towards a better world for all unless patriarchy is challenged. A few men see this and are willing to embark on the difficult task of challenging the ideology that dehumanizes them as much as it disempowers women.

Feminists have been at the forefront of the critique of the crisis of reproduction and of the environmental crisis:

> Women stand at the crossroads between production and reproduction, economic activity and the care of human beings, and therefore between economic growth and human development. They are the workers in both spheres – those most responsible, and therefore with most at stake, those who suffer the most when the two work at cross-purposes, and those most sensitive to the need for better integration between the two.[4]

The combination of feminist scholarship and feminist activism has in fact fuelled the transformation of the women's movement into a political force with an agenda for social transformation that goes beyond the focus on women's well-being to women's perspectives on every aspect of life. The leadership of the global women's movement is undoubtedly feminist.

A passion for justice Transformational leadership must also feel passionately about social justice for everyone, not just for women, for women cannot be 'saved' in isolation from their families and communities. The passion for justice comes from our consciousness of our connection with other women, and an awareness of the extent to which the marginalization of women's realities and values is part of the bedrock of injustice. Above all, this passion must be grounded in a feminist ethic based on a willingness

> to listen to women for clues as to how they experience and interpret reality, and to use these indicators as guides to construct a vision of a moral universe wherein women's well-being along with everything they cherish is promoted.[5]

Transformational leadership that is feminist would argue that there is no justice for anyone if there is no justice for women.

A commitment to change things Passion must then be matched by action. Clesarly it is possible to feel passionately about injustice without feeling moved to action. The activist is the person who cannot witness injustice without taking action. Feminist activism is an expression of feminist politics. The following are the characteristics of feminist politics:

- understanding patriarchy and power;
- rejecting dichotomies and dualism;
- solidarity with women;
- respecting diversity;
- affirming women's agency.

Understanding patriarchy and power A feminist analysis of patriarchy has helped women to understand the role of culture, ideology and discourse in the subordination and marginalization of women, and the ways in which these operate as 'invisible' sources of power to perpetuate notions of the 'powerlessness' of women. This analysis has enabled women to have a better understanding of the different types of power that operate in patriarchal society, both visible and invisible power.[6]

The combination of this analysis with over fifty years' experience of organizing has enabled feminist leadership to learn that 'power over' can best be countered by

- recognizing the 'invisible' power of ideology behind those with 'power over' and
- drawing on the 'power within' and the 'power with' others in collective action.

This has allowed for an understanding of how to link counter-cultural strategies that are grounded in feminist values, and combine feminist methodologies of consciousness-raising (that lead to individual empowerment) with a social analysis that links the individual's experience of oppression and subordination to the larger structures that oppress larger groups. On the basis of this analysis, women have been able to use the political approaches of coalitions, alliances and campaigns for joint advocacy. Feminists have also used professional-technical approaches, drawing on theoretical and empirical research and critical analysis, to inform advocacy (political as well as technical) in the pursuit of well-defined goals. These methodologies and strategies are described more fully below as 'feminist praxis'.

Rejecting dichotomies and dualism Dichotomies fix antagonistic or oppositional relations and determine how problems are discussed. By rejecting dichotomies, feminist politics finds different entry points for resolving problems by addressing the systemic crises that undermine human security. These alternative entry points are grounded in the real, material conditions of people's lives.

Example 1. Imagine how differently the problem between Israeli and Palestinian people might be solved if the starting point was an acknowlededgment of the need to guarantee freedom from want and freedom from fear to each community.

Example 2. Imagine how differently trade disputes might be solved if the entry point was an acknowledgement that different countries had evolved policies that addressed the particularities of their history, culture, resources, needs, strengths and vulnerabilities, and that these differences needed to be respected.

Solidarity with women Feminist leadership has also relied on gender identification, along with women's cultural practices of sharing and cooperating with each other, to form networks varied in scope and structure to address issues and build solidarity between women of different interests and concerns. Solidarity has become a better word than 'unity' for recognizing and respecting differences.

Respecting diversity Feminism acknowledges that women are not a homogeneous, but rather a diverse group, according to class, race/ethnicity, generation, institutional location, geo-political locale, sexual orientation, historical conditions and culture. As a result of the UN Decade for Women, women have had to find ways of negotiating these differences. What has emerged is a politics that sees diversity as a strength that deepens our understanding of the complexities of life, and allows for a much wider range of methodologies and strategies for addressing shared concerns and 'common differences'.

Affirming women's agency Women's agency and feminist leadership are the key to finding solutions to problems related to the search for human security. Women must have the ability to define the problems that affect their lives and the capacities to find solutions. The solutions that are most credible are those grounded in the values of feminist praxis and methodology – the search for common, basic requirements for human security for each person, community or group.

The renewal and strengthening of the global women's movement must be done through feminist methodologies and praxis.

Building solidarity, starting with the particularities of women's realities Feminist praxis is a process that starts with the individual (i.e. building inner strength/empowerment, consciousness-raising/conscientization) and moves the individual through the 'community' into global public space (by caucusing, coalition building, campaigns) – a combination of counter-cultural and political approaches.

Feminist praxis uses a framework for analysis that builds on diversity, is holistic, and links women's experience of daily life to an analysis of the global policy framework. It seeks 'globality' through a framework of women's human rights that is grounded in values (e.g. respect for the individual and for diversity, rejection of dichotomies, and affirmation of women's agency) rather than being based on social, economic, political and cultural organizational categories. It works through the on-going negotiation of differences between diverse social, cultural, political and economic realities towards common positions based on common values. This is done by:

- *exposing the values underlying neo-liberalism* (which are exploitative of people and the environment);
- *highlighting the linkages* between social, economic, political and cultural conditions;
- *proposing alternative ways* of exercising power and distributing resources, and defining how a society might be organized if it was grounded in feminist values.

A commitment to personal change The final part is the most important, but also the most difficult to articulate. Change must start within us. It has been difficult for me to articulate this without referring to spirituality, which risks being misunderstood. It is not easy to speak of spirituality in the secular women's movement.[7] The mention of the word conjures up institutionalized religion, which is often oppressive and disempowering for women. Certainly the religious fundamentalism that underlies the 9/11 attacks in the USA, the attacks on women in Muslim countries, and the reversal of rights for women of many Christian and Hindu communities, embodies the opposite of the mutuality and respect that we seek.

Like many women, I think that institutionalized religion is often oppressive of women, even when it does not exhibit the extremes of fundamentalism we have witnessed as women's movements have gained in strength. At the same time, it must be acknowledged that religion plays an important role in the lives of many women.

Spirituality also conjures up images of escapism. The personal transformation I envisage is, however, the opposite of this. It is a source of empowerment, a precursor to engagement in the world and political action. Some of the most radical women I know are those who have chosen to struggle for gender justice within the parameters of their religious traditions.

In a paper on 'NGOs, Social Change and the Transformation of Human Relationships', Michael Edwards and Gita Sen conclude that 'social change requires a recognition – and conscious integration – of three bases of change [value systems, institutional processes and subjective states] and three systems of power ... which combine to produce a "social order"'. They note that the most neglected of these three bases is change at the subjective, personal level. While acknowledging that it is 'exceptionally difficult to achieve', they assert, nevertheless, that 'it is rarely possible to generate sustainable changes in human behaviour simply by altering the rules and institutions that govern our lives [and that] personal transformation is essential [for] social change'.

The kind of personal change I envisage is one that would

challenge leadership to recognize shortcomings and contra-dictions[10] within oneself, to be consistent, ethical and honest about one's own limitations while experiencing one's own inner power. Above all, this kind of personal transformation would prevent us from thinking ourselves superior to others and trying to control or dominate others, but would rather help us take responsibility for ourselves and our actions.

There are a number of reasons for doing this 'internal' work.

- Working for social justice is full of risk and we can do it only if we find a source of power within ourselves that does not depend on the approval of others; one that cannot be taken away by external forces. Feminist practice has not yet come up with the philosophy that would allow women to confront the powerful forces pitted against them without placing themselves in jeopardy, or with a way for women to cope with these forces on a daily basis. And yet women do cope with the complexities, contradictions and crises within themselves and in the world around them. Those who have come closest to doing so seem to act out of a deep consciousness of themselves as spiritual entities, linked to a force greater than themselves.
- The nurturing of the spirit within each of us will help strengthen our movement in a number of ways. It will help address major problems of relationships within women's move-ments: the tensions, the pettiness, the power struggles between women which stem from insecurity and low self-esteem, from competition over men and scarce resources, factors which lead too many to say 'women are their own greatest enemy'.
- The process of spiritual growth also helps us to relinquish the need to control others, and recognize that all we can control is ourselves and our responses to any situation.
- In addition, although we may not talk about it, many of us know that if our work were not grounded in an awareness of the spirit within us, we could not continue. Those who work for social justice for women risk all manner of misrepresenta-tion, ridicule and even the loss of family, friends and livelihood itself. Some risk their lives. We need to find that power within

that sustains us through all the disappointments and betrayals that are an inevitable part of struggle.

- We need to liberate ourselves from the internalization of our own oppression. Third World authors like Frantz Fanon and Paulo Freire have written powerfully about internalized oppression in relation to racism, colonialism and class. Women's consciousness-raising groups have developed a praxis that has helped women to liberate themselves from 'mental slavery' (as in the Bob Marley song).
- Finally, as Alda Facio puts it,
- We need the spiritual to create a feminist movement that offers pleasure to women: sexual pleasure, bodily pleasure, mental pleasure, pleasure of the soul, and also pleasure in work and in activism. We do not need a feminist movement that kills us with work but a movement that dances, laughs, and delights in the creation of choreographics against globalization.[11]

Where might feminist leadership be found?

The answer is: at many levels and in many different spaces. Our experience over the past thirty years suggests a dynamic process of moving forwards and backwards, between local and global, between 'women's spaces' and engagement with mainstream NGOs and movements and governmental agencies wherever action is motivated by feminist politics. As stated in Chapter 2, feminist politics can be found within government bureaucracies and academia no less than in women's organizations or grassroots or global movements.

For the purpose of considering feminist leadership within the global women's movement, however, I will limit myself to considering expressions of leadership in international spaces – conferences and social movements. I start with those within the larger movements for global justice before considering women's spaces.

The World Social Forum (WSF) and Movements for Global Justice (MGJ) For engagement with mainstream NGOs, the World Social Forum is certainly the space that has captured the imagination since the turn of the century. Its recent merger with the anti-war movement has strengthened it; women are a part of this larger movement, and are present in large numbers at the WSF, as well as in demonstrations and protests against the war.

However, with their overwhelming crowds, simple slogans and easily understood banners, these demonstrations and campaigns are not the spaces for dialogue. Neither is the Forum the space for the negotiations that have to take place with men, and some women, on issues of sexism within the social movements. These negotiations are crucial, since sexism will always subvert the more humane, equitable and democratic world these men and women claim to seek. While feminists have begun to negotiate space on organizing committees at regional and international levels, and on panels and plenaries at the Forums, these spaces do not lend themselves to the kind of discussions that might challenge male privilege and change hearts and minds, much as they might raise issues, question assumptions and propose alternative approaches for future exploration.

Women's conferences Women's spaces at international level have included international women's conferences, those organized by the UN as well as by autonomous women's groups. These spaces become all the more important today as we face a more hostile environment. Indeed, even as new space opens up for women's networks within the larger movement for global justice, we need women's spaces for working out our own analyses and issues, for without clarity and coherence among ourselves we will be handicapped in our engagement with the larger movement.

Currently, there is widespread recognition of the limitations and dangers of giving priority to another UN conference – a Fifth World Conference on Women. But there are other international women's conferences. One such space is the International Forum of AWID. AWID's transformation[12] from a US association with strong institutional links, previously known as WID (a technical-professional space) into an international, movement-oriented association – a political space that is also counter-cultural – allows for the kind of networking and organizing that UN conferences afforded. Another such conference is the International Interdisciplinary Congress of Women. There are also numerous gatherings organized by feminist academics and other professionals. The International Association for Feminist Economics (IAFE) and the International Conference of Women Lawyers are examples. All provide space for showcasing new ideas, theorizing, caucusing, coalition and alliance building, and networking – in short, for movement building.

Some women are arguing for an international women's conference on the 'state of the world' (as distinct from a world conference on women). Clearly this cannot be held under the auspices of the UN, where governments determine and control the agenda. My own view is that such a conference is crucial, given the present intensification of pressures on people and the environment. However, a great deal of thought would have to be given to the agenda and the preparatory process.

Experience tells us that the potential of women's conferences for reaching conclusions that can take us to another level in our search for solutions to the problems that concern us depends on the quality of the work that takes place before the conferences. These preparations include small strategy sessions among feminists in leadership positions in the various networks and movements.

They also include the willingness of this leadership to confront contradictions and inconsistencies in their own work and lives, acknowledging asymmetries of power in terms of class, race and nationality as part of a process of personal transformation. Once again it is in small groups, where differences can be negotiated and alliances built, that feminist leadership renews itself.

How might feminist leadership be renewed and strengthened?

We must start with ourselves, in small groups, with women we know well and trust. These groups can be at local, national, regional or global level. Drawing on our experience of organizing over the past thirty years, we know that the work of renewal cannot take place in the fray of conferences.

If the global women's movement is to be effective in the larger movement for global justice, its leadership must return to the basics, working backwards, from the conferences and campaigns, to coalition and alliance-building, from caucusing to the consciousness-raising groups and circles of friendship that enable us to undertake this work without losing our health and humanity. Friendships formed in the process of feminist struggle have helped renew, strengthen and sustain many women.

The special role of leadership at the global level

Women in leadership positions need to understand the global context, to analyse the 'big picture' so we can see more clearly what needs to be done at local level and feed this in at the global level. The global women's movement can give leadership in this.

Within the context of today's globalized world, local and regional movements must locate their work with a clear understanding of the changing global context. However, a global women's movement has a special role to play in creating spaces where the intellectual and strategic work necessary for the strengthening of local movements can take place. The particular strength of a global women's movement is its capacity to act as a focal point for linking women from different localities and producing analyses and strategies that draw on regional differences and strengths. While the legitimacy of a global women's movement depends on its connection to local movements, the role of a global women's movement in catalysing women's action and mobilizing women from around the world to address the present crisis cannot be dismissed.

Leadership institutes play an important role in this. The Center for Women's Global Leadership at Rutgers University is one such space that functions at the global level. Chapters 4 and 6 described how this centre helped formulate the campaign that put 'women's rights as human rights' on the agenda of the International Conference on Human Rights. DAWN's Training Institute in Feminist Advocacy, which focuses on 'linking the themes of gender justice, economic justice and democracy', is another. There are also similar institutes at regional and local levels.

Conclusion

Today the global women's movement stands at the crossroads between protecting hard-won gains and being swept away by the tidal wave of globalization. It is my belief that feminist politics and praxis hold the key to addressing the threat this terrifying conjuncture poses for human security everywhere. Because the forces of globalization impinge most severely on women, it is possible to trace their origins in the social relations of gender grounded in a patriarchy that is racist, that dichotomizes good and evil, production and reproduction, rationality and intuition, male and female; that seeks conformity and robs women of agency.

If the resolution to the crisis depends on women's agency, then the struggle for global justice must include a struggle for women's agency. Women's movements have the experience, the power and the networks for moving forwards. Without denying our differences, I believe that the global women's movement must put them aside, believe in ourselves, and link our efforts to those of others who share the belief that there is no peace or security without a justice that guarantees justice for women.

> We have chosen each other
> and the edge of each other's battles
> the war is the same
> if we lose
> someday women's blood will congeal
> upon a dead planet
> if we win
> there is no telling
> we seek beyond history
> for a new and more possible meeting.
>
> *Audre Lorde*

Notes

1 This vision, taken from a statement prepared by a group of feminists meeting at a Workshop on Feminist Strategies held at the Women's University of Norway in July 2001, is similar to that articulated in DAWN's platform document, *Development Crises and Alternative Visions: Third World Women's Perspectives*, and countless others. It

is likely recognizable as a 'feminist vision'. See Sen and Grawn (1976), pp. 80–1, for the source of this vision.

2 Vandana Shiva makes a useful distinction between capitalist and cultural patriarchy. Cultural patriarchy is 'mediated through cultural oppression' while capitalist patriarchy 'mediates first and foremost through material exploitation and dispensability ... 'one [capitalist patriarchy] hits right at your chances of survival; [cultural patriarchy] narrows the options of how much you can travel, how much of your body you can expose etc. etc. But it doesn't get to the very basis of survival and deny it to large numbers of people, particularly large numbers of women and children all over the world.' In Cindy Duffy and Craig Benjamin (1995), 'Creative Principles: Fighting Capitalism and Patriarchy on a World Scale: An Interview with Vandana Shiva', in World Transformation: Gender, Work and Solidarity in the Era of Free Trade and Structural Adjustment, Shareright rhiZone, pp. 123–33.

3 The traditional feminist critique of the family (developed from Engels) has been qualified by feminists from the experience of the family in different cultural settings. For example, feminist research attributes the higher self-esteem of black girls in the USA to socialization within the black family. This echoes research on families in some Eastern European countries under communism.

4 DAWN (1995), Marker on the Way: The DAWN Debates on Alternative Development, p. 21 (see DAWN website).

5 Elizabeth A. Johnson (1992), p. 67.

6 See Valerie Miller (2001).

7 I am particularly grateful to Alda Facio for writing about a feminist political spirituality in her contribution to The Future of Women's Rights, edited by Joanna Kerr and Ellen Sprenger.

8 Edwards and Sen (2000).

9 'Economic power [as] expressed in the distribution of productive assets and the workings of markets and firms; social power [as] expressed in the status and position awarded to different social groups; and political power [as] define[d by] each person's voice in decision-making in both the private sphere and public affairs.'

10 Especially those of class and race.

11 Kerr et al. (2004), p. 286.

12 This story must be told some day, as an example of institutional transformation.

10 | Epilogue: is another world possible?

The impetus for my writing this book was the war in Iraq; and as I approach the final review of the manuscript I am caught up the crisis in Haiti. What do these two crises tell us about the role of a global women's movement in the larger frame of civil society?

The story told in this book is of a civil society that is relatively benign, that occupied spaces at national and international levels that were relatively open and where progressive positions could be negotiated, sometimes successfully.

In the past few years, the concept of trans-national civil society has received increasing attention, in the hope that it might prevail against the forces of neo-liberal globalization that threaten the security of the majority of the world's people. However, after 9/11, the impressive mobilization of civil society against the war in Iraq was powerless to change the resolve of the most powerful coalition in the world to go to war against Iraq. Moreover, in the context of the 'war on terrorism', trans-national civil society itself is being weakened by the closing off of spaces for dissent.

However, in Haiti we witnessed the opposite: a well organized civil society stood in opposition to a democratically elected President, whose election in the late 1990s symbolized hope for the majority of Haitians (among the most economically deprived people in the Western hemisphere). In the case of Iraq, civil society fails to stop the war; in the case of Haiti, civil society triumphs with the US removal of President Aristide. The example of Haiti shows how easy it is, in certain circumstances, for civil society to be co-opted by, or complicit with, the agendas of superpowers; Iraq shows how difficult it is to stand against the agenda of superpowers. The lesson is that, when civil society organizes to challenge the status quo, it can succeed only when that status quo is in accordance with the interests of global capital.

The conflicts in Iraq and Haiti cannot be fully understood outside the systemic parameters of class and race. Haiti does not have rich resources of oil to which the powerful might lay claim. However, the forces against Aristide seem to have very similar class and race positions to those pitted against Iraq.

Where does a global women's movement feature in this? In Haiti, a collective of women's organizations denounces a statement by a group of women from the Caribbean and the Caribbean diaspora condemning the US-backed coup and calling on CARICOM governments to press for an enquiry into the circumstances surrounding Aristide's removal from Haiti. This collective is part of a broad mobilization of civil society organizations, many supported by US funds, against President Aristide.

The international media tell one story about Haiti; grassroots women from Haiti tell another. We know enough about the history of Haiti – the first black republic to throw off the shackles of slavery and win independence from France, 200 years ago – to understand that we are witnessing a struggle for power in a society that is extremely polarized by class and race. At this time there is no solidarity between women who wish to defend President Aristide and those who wish to see him leave Haiti for ever.

President Aristide is by no means perfect. Among other things, he is alleged to have been complicit in serious abuses of human rights by the armed gangs on which he depended for security. At the same time, a small but well-armed rebel force has been creating chaos in the country, paving the way for the deployment of contingents of US, French and Canadian forces.

The situation in Iraq is just as complex, although there is no question about the violence meted out by Saddam Hussein to his opponents. Deep divisions between his supporters and the Shia majority pit women against each other. But is occupation by the US-led coalition acceptable to the majority of Iraqis? And what does a global women's movement have to say about this when, as in the case of Haiti, women's rights are abused by all sides?

The attacks of 9/11, the bombing of Afghanistan, the assault on Iraq and the 'war against terrorism', the on-going cycle of violence between the Israeli army and the suicide bombers, have all served to highlight the violence that prevails in a world ruled by an aggressive patriarchy. The use of dualisms of good and evil, democratic and undemocratic, civilized and anarchic to contrast the characteristics of the USA and its Western 'allies' (including Israel), and Afghanistan, Iraq and the Palestinians, mask an extreme patriarchy underlying the postures on all sides.

The experiences of Iraq and Haiti draw attention to the need for the global women's movement to rethink its strategies in relation to sexism, racism and class privilege within its own ranks.

Robin Morgan (1984) and many others have noted the sexualized imagery around domination, terrorism and war, and Michael Kaufman[1] has highlighted the link between definitions of masculinity and the war against Iraq by pointing out that this kind of aggression is

> embedded in the psyches of men ... in qualities that far too many men have learned to value, embedded in our political, social and religious cultures ... [where men] admire their ability to kill far more than the ability to give or nurture life ... celebrat[ing] a destructive brand of masculinity far more than the tender feelings they associate with femininity and which, apparently, they have come to despise.

Kaufman has also drawn attention to the way in which these appeals to widespread and acceptable definitions of manhood serve the purposes of those who wish to

> mobilize public opinion and vast resources to unleash so much destruction. They are able to tap into a reservoir of fear of impotency and a love of a triumphant masculinity, and turn these towards their own economic and political ends.

There can be no clearer evidence of this than the words of Colin Powell to the Security Council on 9 March 2003:

> The Security Council must not be *afraid* to take action ... it must not be *impotent* in the face of the threat of Saddam Hussein's possession of weapons of mass destruction. (emphasis mine)

If the words of choice used to strengthen resolve ('manhood') are couched in terms of being 'afraid' and threats of impotence, no one can doubt the sexism that underlies the appeal.

Most people recognize that 'this war heralds a period of even greater international instability for which, we will be told, more arms and more war will be required' (Kaufman). Few recognize that women (especially those living in Islamic countries) and people of colour (especially those of Arab and Asian descent) are most in jeopardy from sexist and racist policies that fuel extremism.

Most people recognize that poverty and injustice create deep resentments making it possible for extremists to recruit the disenfranchised for their deadly projects. Few recognize the sexism inherent in systems that invest in killing rather than in caring. Shifting priorities to the long-term needs of children and the nurturing of communities requires a commitment to redistributive justice. Issues of class and race must be addressed no less than those of sexism. A global women's movement that addresses the ways in which unequal power relations have divided women and kept them from the sisterhood they claim in the face of exclusion and subordination, and that challenges sexism while seeking new definitions of manhood, has something to contribute to our understanding of these issues. Women's movements may not yet be powerful enough to stop the wars, but they can point out the ways to peace, and bear witness to the possibilities of a world

> where basic needs become basic rights and where poverty and all forms of violence are eliminated. [Where] women's values of nurturance and solidarity will characterize human relationships [and where] women's reproductive role will be redefined: child care will be shared by men, women, and society as a whole.[2]

The present crisis throws into relief the connections between sexism, racism and imperialism. It urgently requires dialogue among those who seek global justice. Haiti and Iraq remind us that the greatest contribution a global women's movement might make is to take leadership in addressing sexism and racisim in its own ranks, and encouraging women everywhere to do so.

A global women's movement can also contribute to a new

dialogue about prioritizing 'caring not killing' – the slogan of the Global Women's Strike. A global women's movement can insist that this dialogue must be grounded in women's reality, women's interests in the relationships and conditions that allow for reproduction. What women want is not something very different from what men want: the satisfaction of basic needs for food, shelter, dignity and personal safety; the capacity to provide for their children; and opportunities to express themselves creatively. The difference is that these needs must be the point of the dialogue. If the dialogue continues to be about the relative power of different weapon systems, or about the merits of different forms of violence, or of the choices between one dictator or another, the cycle of violence and deprivation will continue.

The situation in Haiti raises a number of questions about the capacity of a movement based only on gender identity to deal with the larger project of social justice. Unless women deal with issues of class and race as seriously as they address patriarchy, women's movements will not have the credibility to speak of social justice. To facilitate this process the movement might start by addressing four questions.

1. Can a global women's movement built through the leadership of Third World women help articulate an analysis that shows clearly the consequences for everyone of an imperialism that is sexist and racist?
2. Can a global women's movement that struggles through processes of confrontation and negotiation towards respect for difference and diversity offer alternatives to systems – political, economic, social and cultural – based on intolerance of difference and hegemonic ambitions?
3. Can a global women's movement deeply committed to the elimination of violence and poverty challenge systems that glorify violence and exploitation (based on patriarchal definitions of masculinity, racist definitions of civility, and class privilege) in the quest for socio-economic development?
4. Can a global women's movement infused with shared values of caring, compassion, justice and solidarity find ways to per-

suade women and men that their only hope of a more humane world lies in challenging the divisions of gender, class, race and ethnicity that deny social, economic and political and civil rights to others?

Within the context of a movement for global justice that brings the new peace movement together with those working to challenge the economic fundamentalism of neo-liberalism, a global women's movement that addresses contradictions of race, ethnicity and class within its own ranks can serve as a catalyst for women's movements everywhere. Beyond this, we need to articulate a clearer analysis of the links between our gender relations and the systemic and persistent crises in social reproduction, human security and governance, Finally, we need to build a partnership with men who understand that only new models of manhood and womanhood will end the madness that jeopardizes us all.

Notes

1 Michael Kaufman, 'Manhood and War', <www.michael kaufman.com>.

2 Sen and Grown (1987), p. 80.

Bibliography

Basu, Amrita (ed.) (1995) *The Challenge of Local Feminisms: Women's Movements in Global Perspective*, Boulder, CO: Westview Press.

Batiliwala, Srilatha, and David Brown (eds), *Claiming Global Power: Transnational Civil Society and Global Governance*, Massachusetts: Kumarian Press.

Bertell, Rosalie (1985) *No Immediate Danger: Prognosis for a Radioactive Earth*, London: Women's Press.

Bhavnani, Kum-Kum, John Foran and Priya Kurian (2003) *Feminist Futures: Re-imagining Women, Culture and Development*, London: Zed Books.

Braig, Marianne and S. Wolte (eds) (2002) *Common Ground or Mutual Exclusion? Women's Movements and International Relations*, London: Zed Books.

Bunch, Charlotte (1987) *Passionate Politics: Essays 1968–1986, Feminist Theory in Action*, New York: St Martin's Press.

Bunch, Charlotte and N. Reilly (1994) *Demanding Accountability: The Global Campaign and Vienna Tribunal for Women's Human Rights*, New Brunswick, NJ: Center for Women's Global Leadership.

Chesler, M and J. Crowfoot (1992) *Visioning Change*, Michigan: University of Michigan.

Correa, Sonia, with Rebecca Reichmann (1994) *Population and Reproductive Rights: Feminist Perspectives from the South*, London: Zed Books.

Edwards, Michael and John Gaventa (2001) *Global Citizen Action*, Boulder CO: Lynne Reinner Publishers.

Edwards, Michael and Gita Sen (2000) 'NGOs, Social Change and theTransformation of Human Relationships: A 21st Century Civic Agenda', *Third World Quarterly*, 21(4): 605–16.

Fraser, S. Arvonne (1987) *The UN Decade for Women: Documents And Dialogue*, Boulder, CO, and London: Westview Press.

hooks, bell (1994) *Teaching to Transgress*, London: Routledge.

Kerr, Joanna, Ellen Sprenger and Alison Symington (eds) (2004) *The Future of Women's Rights*, London: Zed Books.

Lorde, Audre (1984, 11th printing 1996) *Sister Outsider: Essays and Speeches by Audre Lord*, Freedom, CA: Crossing Press.

Miles, Angela (1996) *Integrative Feminisms: Building Global Visions 1960s–1990s*, New York and London: Routledge.

Miller, Valerie (2001) 'On Politics, Power and People: Lessons from Gender Advocacy, Action and Analysis', Paper presented at On Democracy and Active Citizen Engagement: Best Practices in Advocacy and Networking, Symposium, August, Coady International Institute, St Francis Xavier University, Antigonish, Nova Scotia.

Mohanty, Chandra Talpade, Ann Russo and Lourdes Torres (eds) (1991) *Categories of Struggle: Third World Women and the Politics of Feminism*, Bloomington, IN: Indiana University Press.

Mohanty, Chandra Talpade and M. Jacqui Alexander (eds) (1997) *Feminist Genealogies, Colonial Legacies, Democratic Futures*, New York and London: Routledge.

Morgan, Robin (1984) *Sisterhood is Global: The International Women's Movement Anthology*, New York: Anchor Books Oxfam.

— (2003) Gender and Development: *Women Reinventing Globalization*, May, 11(1).

Petchesky, Rosalind Pollack (2003) *Global Prescriptions: Gendering Health and Human Rights*, London: Zed Books.

Sen, Gita and C. Grown (1976) *Development, Crises and Alternative Visions: Third World Women's Perspectives*, New York: Monthly Review Press.

Shiva, Vandana (1992) *Staying Alive: Women, Ecology and Development*, London: Zed Books.

Smith, Bonnie G. (ed.) (2000) *Global Feminisms Since 1945*, New York and London: Routledge.

Society for International Development (SID) Journal (2001) *Development*, special issue on 'On the Politics of Place', Rome: SID

Suares Toro, Maria (2000) *Women's Voices on Fire – Feminist International Radio Endeavor*, Austin, TX: Anomaly Press.

Taylor, Viviene (2000) *Marketization of Governance*, London: Zed Books.

Waring, Marilyn (1952) *If Women Counted: A New Feminist Economics*, San Francisco, CA: Harper and Row

Selected women's networks and websites

Single-issue networks

Women's Human Rights
- Women's Human Rights Network: http://www.whrnet.org
- International Gay and Lesbian Human Rights Commission: http://www.iglhrc.org
- Center for Women's Global Leadership: http://www.cwgl.rutgers.edu

Sexual and Reproductive Health and Rights
- Center for Reproductive Rights: http://www.reproductiverights.org
- International Women's Health Coalition: http://www.iwhc.org

Violence Against Women
- Family Violence Prevention Fund: http://endabuse.org
- Global Alliance Against Trafficking in Women: http://www.thai.net/gaatw

Environment
- Women Environment and Development Organization (WEDO): http://www.wedo.org

Trade
- International Gender and Trade Network (IGTN): http://www.genderandtrade.net

Peace
- The Global Women's Strike (GWS) http://womenstrike8m.server101.com

Multiple-issue networks

- DAWN: http://www.dawn.org.fj

- Sisterhood is Global Institute (SIGI):
  http://www.sigi.org
- Association for Women's Rights and Development:
  http://www.awid.org
- Women's International Coalition for Economic Justice:
  http://www.wicej.org
- Women Environment and Development Organization (WEDO)
  http://www.wedo.org

Communications
- International Women's Tribune Centre: http://www.iwtc.org
- Isis International – Chile: http://www.isis.cl
- Isis International – Manila: http://www.isiswomen.org

Appendix I

The World Needs the Love of a Free Woman
Nan Peacocke, November 1985

The world needs the love of a free woman
not the love of a good woman
there's already too much
of that good woman's love
waiting
in the bantustans
while her husband's soul is mined
deep in South Africa

Enough of the love of a good woman
far in the dark city
at a high small window
lying on a bed
crying in her sleep
so she won't disturb the others.

The world has seen and seen the one
who keeps these things in her heart
she kneels
beholding the bleeding feet
of her boy
Blesed Art Thou Among Women
and never a nuisance.

The world needs the love of a free woman
who forgives god
but doesn't ask him for an explanation
of her brother's murder
her daughter's rape
her mother's unrepresented life

She speaks loud
naming lies
she moves

clearing the piercing forest
of guns and crosses held aloft
she works
planting hopes
and fetching from the horizon
the thoughts of free women
rising in millions
from this shantytown.

Appendix 2: The Global Women's Strike

The Global Women's Strike was born when women in Ireland asked the International Wages for Housework Campaign (WfH) to support their call for a women's strike on 8 March 2000, and WfH made the Irish Strike global.

In fact the Strike began in 1952 with Selma James's little pamphlet called *A Woman's Place* and continued with her *Power of Women and the Subversion of the Community* (1972), and *Sex, Race and Class* (1973). It was previously assumed that only waged workers, mainly men in industrial countries, were 'real' workers, and that only they could change the world. The Campaign broke with this sexism and racism, establishing autonomy as a new basis for organising. It made the case that the work women do for wages is a second job, on top of unwaged work in the home and in the community, producing all the workers of the world.

Since then, we have been campaigning for recognition and wages for all unwaged work, as well as for pay equity – joint levers against women's poverty, exploitation and discrimination of every kind. In Beijing in 1995, the International Women Count Network which WfH coordinates, supported by more than 2000 organisations and with CARICOM taking the lead in negotiations between governments, won the UN decision that national accounts should include how much unwaged work women do and its economic value. Trinidad & Tobago and Spain have put this into law, while other countries are doing time-use surveys, and increasingly consider unwaged work in court decisions and government policies.

The Strike has brought together women in over 60 countries, including grassroots organisations with impressive track records. From taking action together every 8 March, it has grown to a global network that strengthens the ongoing daily struggles of grassroots women (and men).

In Venezuela, we work with the women who are building a

caring economy and who won Article 88 of the revolutionary Constitution, which recognises housework as an economic activity that creates added value and produces social welfare and wealth, entitling housewives to social security.

The Strike is part of the movement against war and occupation. With the theme INVEST IN CARING NOT KILLING, we demand that the $1 trillion now spent on military budgets annually goes instead for basic survival needs, and therefore for women the first carers and fighters for the survival of loved ones: clean accessible water, food security, healthcare, housing, education, safety from rape and other violence, protection of our planet. We claim for a start the US military budget – over half of all military spending – with which 'Corporate America' imposes its economic and political interests on the whole world (including on people in the US).

The struggle women make for ourselves and our communities is often as ignored as the unwaged survival work we do, including growing most of the world‚s basic food. The Strike gives visibility to women of colour – including women of Indigenous, African and Asian descent – single mothers, women with disabilities, immigrant women, sex workers, lesbian women, to spell out their contribution to every economy, society and struggle.

We work with Payday – men who actively support our struggle because they agree that INVEST IN CARING NOT KILLING is the priority of all workers and all humanity. Men owe women their daily survival – from breastfeeding to cooked meals, clean clothes and emotional support; they also depend on women opposing the values of the Market that now threaten everyone's survival.

The Strike is neither party political, nor separatist. It is ambitious for the movement for change but it stands against personal ambition that undermines mutual accountability. The Strike is a framework for unity – among sectors of women, between women and men within and among countries – because it is based on each sector's independent struggle – the basis for a truly diverse movement from the bottom up.

Andaiye, Guyana,
June 2004

Appendix 3: The Sisterhood is Global Institute

The Sisterhood is Global Institute, celebrates its 20th anniversary in November 2004. My inclusion in the list of women invited by Robin Morgan to contribute to the book, Sisterhood is Global, gave me my first inkling of a trans-national movement, and my first sense that I had something to contribute to it. It was probably the same for many of the other contributors.

In recording the achievements of the Institute over the years, its founder, Robin Morgan writes:

> The Sisterhood Is Global Institute has a record of which we can be extremely proud. It has blazed a great many paths over the past 20 years – and I want to preserve and honor that institutional memory.

- We sent out the first Urgent Action Alerts focused on female human rights, and created the first grassroots feminist international activist base – the Sisterhood is Global Network (SIGNET) for mail, fax, phone, and (later on) email campaigns (under the Presidency of Maria de Lourdes Pintasilgo and Executive Directorship of Karen Berry).
- We raised the vital global issue of women's unpaid labor and the invisibility of that labor in national accounts and censuses, and convened the first Global Women's Leadership Assembly (when the Institute, presided over by Marilyn Waring, was based in New Zealand/Aotearoa).
- We were the first multi-issue women's INGO to establish programs with women in Muslim societies as a feminist priority, situating the first SIGI branch office in Amman, Jordan, as well as creating and publishing Women's Rights Manuals specifically for that constituency – in Azeri, Arabic, Bangla, English, Farsi,

French, Hindi, Malay, Urdu, Uzbek, and Russian (during the tenure of Mahnaz Afkhami).

- The two-week-long Sisterhood is Global Institute Dialogues, which took place in five cities across The Philippines (organized by Filipina SIGI member Anna Leah Sarabia) produced a major conference in Manila and a subsequent book.
- Sisterhood is Global Institute panels and presentations have been featured at every UN World Conference on Women, and Sisterhood Is Global Institute fact-finding missions have their own illustrious record: members visiting, working with, and publicizing the priorities of women in Afghanistan, Austria, Australia, Brazil, the Caribbean, China, Egypt, Greece, Honduras, Indonesia, Italy, Israel, Japan, Jordan, Kenya, Lebanon, Namibia, Nepal, Norway, Pakistan, Palestine (Gaza and West Bank), Rwanda, South Africa, Spain, Thailand, the United Kingdom, the United States, Uzbekistan, the former Yugoslavia, and Zambia.
- Operating from the conviction, articulated at our founding, that all issues are 'women's issues', the Institute has been active on a wide range of subjects. A sampling would include: facilitating funding for the first conference on the status of old women in India (convened by SIGI member Sonal Shukla); exploring the economic and environmental impact of declining fisheries on fisherwomen globally; investigating sex tourism, trafficking, and slavery in Thailand; furthering research on FGM; and starting a tradition of 'Peace Cafés' to encourage dialogue between adversarial groups (indigenous and/or refugee) in Canada.

The number and variety of activities of the Institute gives a sense of the vision of the women who took initiatives in those early days at the start of the UN Decade for Women.

Index

197

Forum '85, 56–8; Peace Tent, 58
Foucault, Michel, 131
Fraser, Nancy, 141
free trade, rejection of, 89
Freire, Paulo, 175
fundamentalism, 55, 115, 121; campaign against, 5; economic, 100; religious, 173 (growth of, 99, 100; in USA, 100, 103); rise of, 76; spread of, 71–2
funding, external, dependence on, 155

gender, 103; and trade, 90
gender equity, resistance to, 130
gender identity, 11
gender-blindness of data, 72
genetically modified organisms, 84
global, use of term, 1
Global Campaign for Women's Human Rights (GCWHR), 117, 118–19
global reach of women's movements, 17–18
Global Tribunal on Violations of Women's Human Rights, 92–3, 119
globality, and women's movement, 18
globalization, 68, 147, 154, 179
glocality, use of term, 20
governance: crisis of, 139, 160; good, 101; marketization of, 101
grassroots movements, 154
Group of 77 (G77), 30–1, 43, 97–8
Group of 8 (G-8), 4
Grown, Caren, 75

Haiti, 7, 139
Hall, Stuart, 142
Health Empowerment, Rights and Accountability (HERA), 98
HIV–AIDS, 147; young women as victims of, 148
hooks, bell, 14, 144
Hoskins, Fran, 38
human rights, 104, 113, 122, 152; of women, 89, 91, 117, 141, 159, 178

human rights movement, 33
human rights paradigm, shift to, 103

identity politics, 11, 71, 155
ideology, invisible power of, 170
import-substitution industrialization (ISI), 30, 69
impregnation, forced, 94
independence movements, 28
India, environmental issues in, 84
indigenous peoples, 87, 145
information technologies: as tool of struggle, 46; enable networking, 137, 156
institutionalization versus autonomy, 156
Integrated Rural Development, 30, 69
integrating women in development, 78
Inter-American Commission on the Status of Women (CIM), 33
International Alliance of Women, 33
International Association for Feminist Economics (IAFFE), 177
International Conference of Women Lawyers, 177
International Conference on Human Rights (Vienna, 1993), 18, 88, 91, 178
International Conference on Population and Development (ICPD) (Cairo 1994), 32, 81, 88, 96, 97–8, 115; Platform of Action, 98, 102
International Council of Women, 33
International Day Against Violence Against Women, 14
international financial institutions (IFIs), 29, 74
International Gender and Trade Network (IGTN), 89–90
international instruments, domesticating of, 124
International Interdisciplinary Congress of Women, 14, 116, 177
International Labour Organization (ILO), 30
International Monetary Fund (IMF),

Index

Participating organizations

Both ENDS A service and advocacy organization that collaborates with environment and indigenous organizations, both in the South and in the North, with the aim of helping to create and sustain a vigilant and effective environmental movement.

Nieuwe Keizersgracht 45, 1018 VC Amsterdam, The Netherlands
tel: +31 20 623 0823 fax: +31 20 620 8049
e-mail: info@bothends.org
website: www.bothends.org

Catholic Institute for International Relations (CIIR) CIIR aims to contribute to the eradication of poverty through a programme that combines advocacy at national and international level with community-based development.

Unit 3 Canonbury Yard, 190a New North Road, London N1 7BJ, UK
tel: +44 (0)20 7354 0883 fax: +44 (0)20 7359 0017
e-mail: ciir@ciir.org
website: www.ciir.org

Corner House The Corner House is a UK-based research and solidarity group working on social and environmental justice issues in the North and South.

PO Box 3137, Station Road, Sturminster Newton, Dorset DT10 1YJ,
UK
tel: +44 (0)1258 473795 fax: +44 (0)1258 473748
e-mail: cornerhouse@gn.apc.org
website: www.cornerhouse.icaap.org

Council on International and Public Affairs (CIPA) CIPA is a human rights research, education and advocacy group, with a particular focus on economic and social rights in the USA and elsewhere around the world. Emphasis in recent years has been given to resistance to corporate domination.

777 United Nations Plaza, Suite 3C, New York, NY 10017, USA
tel: +1 212 972 9877 fax: +1 212 972 9878
e-mail: cipany@igc.org
website: www.cipa-apex.org

Dag Hammarskjöld Foundation The Dag Hammarskjöld Founda-tion, established in 1962, organizes seminars and workshops on social, economic and cultural issues facing developing countries, with a particular focus on alternative and innovative solutions. Results are published in its journal *Develpment Dialogue*.

Övre Slottsgatan 2, 753 10 Uppsala, Sweden.
tel: +46 18 102772 fax: +46 18 122072
e-mail: secretariat@dhf.uu.se
website: www.dhf.uu.se

Development GAP The Development Group for Alternative Policies is a non-profit development resource organization working with popular organizations in the South and their Northern partners in support of a development that is truly sustainable and that advances social justice.

927 15th Street, NW, 4th Floor, Washington, DC 20005, USA
tel: +1 202 898 1566 Fax: +1 202 898 1612
e-mail: dgap@igc.org
website: www.developmentgap.org

Focus on the Global South Focus is dedicated to regional and global policy analysis and advocacy work. It works to strengthen the capacity of organizations of the poor and marginalized people of the South and to better analyse and understand the impacts of the globalization process on their daily lives.

c/o CUSRI, Chulalongkorn University, Bangkok 10330, Thailand
tel: +66 2 218 7363 fax: +66 2 255 9976
e-mail: admin@focusweb.org
website: www.focusweb.org

IBON IBON Foundation is a research, education, and information institution that provides publications and services on socio-economic issues as support to advocacy in the Philippines and abroad. Through its research and databank, formal and non-formal education programs, media work, and international networking, IBON aims to build the capacity of both Philippine and international organizations.

Rm. 303 SCC Bldg., 4427 Int. Old Sta. Mesa, Manila 1008 Philippines
tel: +632 7132729, +632 7132737, +632 7130912 fax: +632 7160108
e-mail: editors@ibon.org
website: www.ibon.org

Inter Pares Inter Pares, a Canadian social justice organization, has been active since 1975 in building relationships with Third World development groups and providing support for community-based development programmes. Inter Pares is also involved in education and advocacy in Canada, promoting understanding about the causes and effects of, and solutions to, poverty.

221 Laurier Avenue East, Ottawa, Ontario, K1N 6P1 Canada
tel: +1 613 563 4801 fax: +1 613 594 4704

Public Interest Research Centre PIRC is a research and campaigning group based in Delhi that seeks to serve the information needs of activists and organizations working on macro-economic issues concerning finance, trade and development.

142, Maitri Apartments, Plot No. 28, Patparganj, Delhi: 110092, India
tel: +91 11 2221081, 2432054 fax: +91 11 2224233
e-mail: kaval@nde.vsnl.net.in

Third World Network TWN is an international network of groups and individuals involved in efforts to bring about a greater articulation of the needs and rights of peoples in the Third World; a fair distribution of the world's resources; and forms of development that are ecologically sustainable and fulfil human needs. Its international secretariat is based in Penang, Malaysia.

121-S Jalan Utama, 10450 Penang, Malaysia
tel: +60 4 226 6159 fax: +60 4 226 4505
e-mail: twnet@po.jaring.my
website: www.twnside.org.sg

Third World Network–Africa TWN–Africa is engaged in research and advocacy on economic, environmental and gender issues. In relation to its current particular interest in globalization and Africa, its work focuses on trade and investment, the extractive sectors and gender and economic reform.

2 Ollenu Street, East Legon, PO Box AN19452, Accra-North, Ghana.
tel: +233 21 511189/503669/500419 fax: +233 21 511188
e-mail: twnafrica@ghana.com

World Development Movement (WDM) The World Development Movement campaigns to tackle the causes of poverty and injustice. It is a democratic membership movement that works with partners in the South to cancel unpayable debt and break the ties of IMF conditionality, for fairer trade and investment rules, and for strong international rules on multinationals.

25 Beehive Place, London SW9 7QR, UK
tel: +44 (0)20 7737 6215 fax: +44 (0)20 7274 8232
e-mail: wdm@wdm.org.uk
website: www.wdm.org.uk

The Global Issues series

Already available in English

Walden Bello, *Deglobalization: Ideas for a New World Economy*

Robert Ali Brac de la Perrière and Franck Seuret, *Brave New Seeds: The Threat of GM Crops to Farmers*

Peggy Antrobus, *The Global Women's Movement: Origins, Issues and Strategies*

Greg Buckman, *Globalization: Tame It or Scrap It?*

Ha-Joon Chang and Ilene Grabel, *Reclaiming Development: An Alternative Economic Policy Manual*

Oswaldo de Rivero, *The Myth of Development: The Non-viable Economies of the 21st Century*

Graham Dunkley, *Free Trade: Myth, Reality and Alternatives*

Joyeeta Gupta, *Our Simmering Planet: What to do about Global Warming?*

Nicholas Guyatt, *Another American Century? The United States and the World since 9.11*

Martin Khor, *Rethinking Globalization: Critical Issues and Policy Choices*

John Madeley, *Food for All: The Need for a New Agriculture*

John Madeley, *Hungry for Trade: How the Poor Pay for Free Trade*

Damien Millet and Eric Toussaint, *Who Owes Who? 50 Questions About World Debt*

A. G. Noorani, *Islam and Jihad: Prejudice versus Reality*

Riccardo Petrella, *The Water Manifesto: Arguments for a World Water Contract*

Peter Robbins, *Stolen Fruit: The Tropical Commodities Disaster*

Toby Shelley, *Oil: Politics, Poverty and the Planet*

Vandana Shiva, *Protect or Plunder? Understanding Intellectual Property Rights*

Harry Shutt, *A New Democracy: Alternatives to a Bankrupt World Order*

David Sogge, *Give and Take: What's the Matter with Foreign Aid?*

Paul Todd and Jonathan Bloch, *Global Intelligence: The World's Secret Services Today*

In preparation

Julian Burger, *First Peoples: What Future?*

Koen De Feyter, *Human Rights: Social Justice in the Age of the Market*

Susan Hawley and Morris Szeftel, *Corruption: Privatization, Transnational Corporations and the Export of Bribery*

Ann-Christin Sjölander Holland, *Water for Sale? Corporations against People*

Paola Monzini, *The Market in Women: Prostitution, Trafficking and Exploitation*

Roger Moody, *Digging the Dirt: The Modern World of Global Mining*

Edgar Pieterse, *City Futures: Confronting the Crisis of Urban Development*

Vivien Stern, *The Making of Crime: Prisons and People in a Market Society*

Nedd Willard, *The War on Drugs: Is This the Solution?*

For full details of this list and Zed's other subject and general catalogues, please write to: The Marketing Department, Zed Books, 7 Cynthia Street, London N1 9JF, UK or e-mail:

sales@zedbooks.demon.co.uk

Visit our website at: http://www.zedbooks.demon.co.uk

This book is also available in the following countries

Egypt MERIC (The Middle East Readers' Information Center) 2 Bahgat Ali Street, Tower D/Apt. 24 Zamalek, Cairo tel: 20 2 735 3818/736 3824 fax: 20 2 736 9355

Fiji University Book Centre, University of South Pacific, Suva tel: 679 313 900 fax: 679 303 265

Ghana EPP Book Services, PO Box TF 490, Trade Fair, Accra tel: 233 21 773087 fax: 233 21 779099

Mauritius Editions Le Printemps, 4 Club Road, Vacoas

Mozambique Sul Sensacoes, PO Box 2242, Maputo tel: 258 1 421974 fax: 258 1 423414

Namibia Book Den, PO Box 3469, Shop 4, Frans Indongo Gardens, Windhoek tel: 264 61 239976 fax: 264 61 234248

Nepal Everest Media Services, GPO Box 5443, Dillibazar, Putalisadak Chowk, Kathmandu tel: 977 1 416026 fax: 977 1 250176

Nigeria Mosuro Publishers, 52 Magazine Road, Jericho, Ibadan tel: 234 2 241 3375 fax: 234 2 241 3374

Pakistan Vanguard Books, 45 The Mall, Lahore tel: 92 42 735 5079 fax: 92 42 735 5197

Papua New Guinea Unisearch PNG Pty Ltd, Box 320, University, National Capital District tel: 675 326 0130 fax: 675 326 0127

Philippines IBON Foundation, Inc., 3rd Floor SCC Bldg., 4427 Int. Old Sta. Mesa, Manila, Philippines 1008 tel: (632) 713-2729 / 713-2737 fax: (632) 716-0108

Rwanda Librairie Ikirezi, PO Box 443, Kigali tel/fax: 250 71314

Sudan The Nile Bookshop, New Extension Street 41, PO Box 8036, Khartoum tel: 249 11 463 749

Tanzania TEMA Publishing Co Ltd, PO Box 63115, Dar Es Salaam tel: 255 51 113608 fax: 255 51 110472

Uganda Aristoc Booklex Ltd, PO Box 5130, Kampala Road, Diamond Trust Building, Kampala tel/fax: 256 41 254867

Zambia UNZA Press, PO Box 32379, Lusaka tel: 260 1 290409 fax: 260 1 253952

Zimbabwe Weaver Press, PO Box A1922, Avondale, Harare tel: 263 4 308330 fax: 263 4 339645